God for Now

God for Now

Theology through Evangelical
and Charismatic Experience

Mark Amos

WIPF & STOCK · Eugene, Oregon

GOD FOR NOW
Theology through Evangelical and Charismatic Experience

Wipf & Stock
An Imprint of Wipf and Stock Publishers
199 W. 8th Ave., Suite 3
Eugene, OR 97401

www.wipfandstock.com

PAPERBACK ISBN: 978-1-7252-5223-3
HARDCOVER ISBN: 978-1-7252-5224-0
EBOOK ISBN: 978-1-7252-5225-7

Manufactured in the U.S.A.   02/21/20

Contents

Preface

I'm not sure who gets to decide, but I think I am an evangelical charismatic Christian. This comes with certain liabilities. Some people say they are open to the charismatic, but are not so willing to say they *are* charismatic. It still sounds a bit wacky; a bit loud; a bit untheological. Also, I am not very "charismatic"—quite the introvert in fact. Still, my preferences include what might be defined as charismatic. "Evangelical" also has connotations. In the minds of some, it is the same word as "fundamentalist" and few people want to be one of those. Certain theological types are happy to be "post-evangelical"; that sounds more hipster; less stuck; friendlier. The term evangelical denotes, amongst other things, believing certain things about Scripture. Unfortunately, discussion of evangelicalism sometimes gets stuck there. But that is not the sum total of the word. It comes from "gospel," the good news. I think Christianity, including the Bible, is good news, and that is why I am writing about it.

This book has evolved slowly. The different sections relate to various pieces I have written or had in mind to write. I wrote some of these in academic contexts. In my Master's thesis I considered the Christologies of Karl Barth and Karl Rahner. The first part of the book relates to and builds upon ideas arrived at there. My unfinished PhD thesis, tackling the problematic matter of divine freedom, relates to the last part. The rest of the book arises from personal reflection of church experience, particularly relating to the charismatic.

I have had very real questions about my faith tradition, but find I still want to be part of it. More than that, I am grateful to be part of the leadership team of my church. I don't blame all my questions on the tradition. Sometimes they are more to do with me. Nevertheless, these questions frame some of what I will say here. The big value of evangelical charismatic Christianity is that it has, at its best, a confidence in speaking about God. This has rubbed off on me, and it means that I speak here unashamedly.

I am also a secondary school teacher. This means that I cannot help wanting to say something relevant to those who are not Christian as well as those who are. Because I do a lot of my theological thinking and talking outside of the church, I approach things in a particular way. I find my vision directed outwards. As much as I expect the audience of this book to be Christian, it is likely that the same audience are working out their faith outside the confines of "church." I hope what I say, therefore, relates meaningfully to Christian witness in the world.

It is worth highlighting a few things that are not in the book, or a few things that this book isn't. It isn't an ecclesiology, as much as many of the theological questions relate to church. It isn't a social agenda, as much as some of my theological thinking has social implications. Finally, it isn't ethics, although there are inevitable ethical implications to any coherently framed theology. I hope to write about these things in due course, but not just now.

Acknowledgments

I HAVE NUMEROUS PEOPLE to thank. Many of the ideas presented here were shaped during my undergraduate studies at Nazarene Theological College in Manchester. It was a great place to study. I will always be grateful to my teachers there.

My master's thesis was supervised by Professor Karen Kilby at the University of Nottingham. She was an excellent supervisor, encouraging and constructive in equal spades. I suspect some of what I say, particularly regarding apophatic theology, diverges from her good tutelage. When it does, it is likely that I have misunderstood apophaticism!

My thanks to Professor Paul Janz who had the unenviable task of supervising my attempted PhD thesis. I embarked upon this whilst working nearly full time as a head of department, and then briefly as an assistant headteacher in a secondary school. No wonder I couldn't propose anything groundbreaking. Nevertheless, it was a hugely valuable experience.

Culham St Gabriel's provided funding and support through both masters and PhD studies. I also had the privilege of completing a Farmington Fellowship at Harris Manchester College that gave me valuable time to work on my master's thesis. The work that both organizations do to support Christian education in schools is hugely valuable.

Various people have been willing to read some of the book during its development. Those from my church: Richard Walker, Sean and Liz Green, and Roy Avis. There were probably others, so apologies to those I've missed. Several people gave significant feedback on the first part: Andy McCullough, Richard McIntosh, John Scott, and Matthew Hosier. Fewer people read parts 2 and 3 and they are probably the poorer for it. Aaron Edwards's suggestions at a late stage were particularly helpful.

ACKNOWLEDGMENTS

Thanks to my department at the Abbey School, particularly Kyle Scott, and to my students, who—sometimes unbeknown to them—engaged with various ideas almost daily. My students are likely to disagree with a good deal of what I say, but they have also shaped the text more than they could know.

Most importantly, thank you to my family: to my dear parents, my beloved and ever-giving wife, and my wonderful boys, each to whom I dedicate this book.

Abbreviations

CD   Barth, Karl. Church Dogmatics. Translated by G. T.
        Thomson et al. Edinburgh: T. & T. Clark, 1936–77.

IJST   International Journal of Systematic Theology

SJT   Scottish Journal of Theology

Introduction

"WHY ARE YOU *STILL* a Christian?" This has to be one of the most important questions going, for Christians at least.[1] It demands an answer—a testimony. Testimonies are popular in the Christianity I have known. We hear them when someone becomes a Christian or has a remarkable answer to prayer. I want to offer a testimony of an altogether more normal, though equally remarkable thing—the ongoing desire to be a Christian—to be Christian *now*; in my case, an evangelical charismatic Christian.

My testimony is positive, but also involves critical questioning. Many of us have questions about our faith and experiences. We bring a certain unsettledness to the table. Here I offer a constructive way of considering the positives of charismatic and evangelical theology whilst acknowledging the problems. Despite everything, I believe we can know God and hence I want to be a Christian. I think I can show why. I will travel over well-worn, and not so well-worn, paths to show this. For those with questions about what they think and feel, I provide a way through. If you are such a person, this book is for you.

There are other things I could be: skeptical, agnostic, spiritual, Buddhist, or plain indifferent. These paths have the advantage of being more culturally acceptable. Nevertheless, I am a Christian *and* want to be. Why is that? My reasons are quite straightforward. I offer three in particular. First, Jesus captivates me, particularly as portrayed in the Gospels. I desire him as the living and breathing reality of God become flesh. Second, I have experienced what I take to be the love of God through encounters with the

---

1. A student asked Rowan Williams "Why are you a Christian?" at a school conference I attended. In response, he said he might give a more interesting answer to the question, "Why are you *still* a Christian?"

Holy Spirit. These encounters have arrested my attention and reconfigured my imagination. They have led to a fresh understanding of who God is: a present and living reality. Third, I believe God knows us and wants to be known today. My confidence comes from what God has said in Christ and through the Spirit.

So this book is really about God. Reasons for being and remaining Christian are given, but what I am getting at, in all hopefulness, is God. This is theology. I want to know God *now*. By, "now," I mean in present experience. The knowing of God relates to things experienced, to questions we have. This is why it is so important to talk from experience.

I understand the problems with my reasons for being Christian. My day job—teaching philosophy and theology in a secondary school—involves pulling reasons like the ones discussed here to pieces. I have read and wrestled with ideas that could have destroyed the foundations of my beliefs. And yet, I am *still* Christian, and want to be.

In what follows, I will explore the reasons mentioned by integrating experience—my experience—with theology. Some say theology and experience are bad bedfellows. I have sympathy. We need not concede everything to experience. Those of us from evangelical traditions feel on safer ground prioritizing Scripture over experience. Scripture is about objective truth, whereas experience is all too subjective. I will explore this problematic relation but insist that consideration of theology and reflection on experience are together vital. They are what forms a particular faith—a living and critically engaged faith. This is true for me. From what I have seen, it is also true for others.

I will interact closely with some theologians, not to be laborious but because their insights relate to my being Christian—to my recognizing God. My particular tradition has tended to advocate popular Reformed evangelical authors.[2] Two distinctive features of their theology continue to underpin my thinking: one, a Reformed understanding of grace; that is, God's unmerited favor and its effects; and two, an emphasis on the emotions, including desire, not least in relation to the charismatic. Although such writers helped spark my interest in theology, I confess to finding theological sustenance in new places these days. It is these theologians that I interact with here. Their contributions pose and address questions I now

2. For a time, key theological influencers for Newfrontiers were people like John Piper and Wayne Grudem. I will occasionally show how I differ from the them, though do not presume to offer a full critique.

burn with. My interactions will be as straightforward as possible, but some serious thinking will be required.

The faith I am giving testimony to, involves critical searching—involves theology. As a result, this book sits between the theological and devotional. The aim is to say something valuable for those who are working out their faith in light of what they have read *and* what they have felt. I not only want to confirm faith but also unsettle it, stir it, and provoke it. What I explore relates both to belief and to doubt and is thus personal. In addressing the question of why one still wants to be Christian, we are in the realm of personal theology. Put differently, this is theology through experience.

To the point in question: the most straightforward reason for still being Christian is being utterly attracted to and undone by the person of Jesus Christ. It is not only the idea of him that draws me but his reality. To put it as directly as I can, I am drawn through my desire, reason and longing to the Christ who leaps out from the pages of Scripture as actually real. There are various motives at play in saying this, but my reasons are honest. I see that it is a big leap from finding Christ appealing to saying what I will also say—that I trust the biblical accounts of him. I will thus need to give an account of why Scripture remains formative for me.

My desire for Christ comes from various experiences. I see Christ everywhere. He has never disappointed. Being as my most profound tie to Christian faith is a continuing enthrallment with Christ, the first part of the book is about him. That said, I give substantial space to how we get from Scripture to Jesus. The second part is about the Holy Spirit. In particular, I will focus on the interaction of theology with charismatic experience. What I have experienced in charismatic worship is an important element to my still being Christian. Nevertheless, some reconciliation needs to take place between charismatic expression and theological reflection. I believe this is possible. In the last part, I consider the implications of an understanding of Christ and the Spirit for knowing God. As already indicated, I feel able to say I am known by God and in turn know God. This conclusion is hopeful and offers cause to be thankful. We are known and loved by God and are in turn enabled to know and love God and each other.

Clarifying "Experience"

Before going any further, I should straighten some things out regarding experience and feeling. If the God I am drawn towards *only* exists in my experience, then this is no God—it is just me. Our understanding of God can therefore never be *reduced* to experience. Likewise, theology should not be an individualistic endeavor, born only out of a particular experience. Faith in God should not be approached through a sense of self-importance or obsessive inwardness. However, the question of why I am still a Christian in terms of my conviction and commitment must reckon in part with such considerations as desire and feelings—with experience.[3]

What we are speaking of is the communicability of the God of the Scriptures—God then and God now. I am not trying to affirm my experience, but open up my way of expressing faith, in order to give an account. There are other reasons to still be a Christian not addressed here. I am not saying, for example, that God's grace has nothing to do with it.[4] Likewise, I am not saying there are no good rational reasons for my faith. However, the present focus is testimony, not rational arguments. This testimony starts with Jesus Christ.

3. Francis Spufford says the following: "I assent to the ideas because I have the feelings; I don't have the feelings because I've assented to the ideas." Spufford, *Unapologetic*, 19. For me, the ideas and the feelings are more connected than this. I came to Spufford's book late, out of fear it would remove the need to write this one. Although brilliant, it didn't.

4. I am sure grace has everything to do with it.

Part 1

Jesus

Introduction

THE CHRIST WHO APPEALS to me aesthetically but also confronts and challenges is the one spoken about in the Bible. Christ is presented at his most vivid and compelling in the gospels. I have known these accounts since childhood and I love the man we read about there. As a young child, I can remember singing:

> There is a green hill far away,
> Without a city wall
> Where our dear Lord was crucified;
> Who died to save us all.[1]

Singing this song is one of my earliest memories. Even then, I was drawn to this faraway hill and the man being crucified there. It seemed full of mystery, and yet it triggered something in my imagination. There was a point of connection. I could see something of Jesus and wanted to know more. I still want to know him more. Even that line "died to save us all" holds so much I want to know more about. He has never ceased to draw me to himself, never ceased to question and move me. It doesn't take much to turn my thoughts to Jesus. If I read a storybook about him with my children, my emotions get straight there: to Galilee by the sea; to the home of a tax collector; to the temple in Jerusalem. The Jesus I know, even from that strange world of old, speaks life into this world, breaks into the moment.

For a number of years, I lived and worked with teenagers living in economic and social deprivation. The Jesus that I have come to know would have understood those teenagers and they would have been drawn to him. Jesus knew what it was to be cast out into the darkness—to be on

---

1. Cecil Frances Alexander, 1848. Public Domain.

3

the underside of humanity.[2] He would have been for them and with them. I have also taught teenagers from economic and social privilege. The Jesus I know would also be for them. He would be their hope and transformation.

In church, I look around and see that Jesus is the object of our worship. When we sing songs that speak of him we are glad. When we gather to eat bread and drink wine, we know him with us. In each of these spaces, Christ has been the center from which everything else makes sense—at least as I have seen it. I seek this same Jesus when reading theology. Studying theology has been a joy and a frustration. It has ignited passion and kept me awake with questions. I couldn't do without it. As I narrate my experience of God, it is as one who feels things through theological reflection. Reading *about* Jesus never gets tiring. He keeps me wanting to be Christian and seeing what theologians have said about him helps. In particular, a number of authors on the gospels enable us to recognize him more fully. They pursue Jesus with intent and heart. We now turn to the wisdom of these commentators whilst maintaining a focus on the motivations of faith.

2. There will be more to say of this later.

1

Christ and Scripture

The Real Jesus?

IN MANY WAYS, THE world of Jesus was not like ours—not completely differ-ent, but different enough to feel strange. We should realize that we often cast Jesus in our likeness. We see him as we see ourselves. We *want* him to be like us. My likeness is white, university educated, English. Jesus was none of the above. To get to him we therefore need to do some work. Context is key. Sometimes doing background work is tough—boring even. However, look-ing into the historical Jesus is never dull. Understanding his world brings him to life. It makes him more interesting, not less. When we catch Jesus as he was in flesh and blood, we see he is not so much the esoteric holy man speaking and acting on some existential plane. He is much more visceral and salt of the earth than that.

We come to see that he is not always the guy we have made him out to be, in art, song, and culture. When we look closer and are ready to have our assumptions challenged, Jesus comes into view. Jesus was, of course, a middle-Eastern Jew. A carpenter from Galilee, no less. This matters, not so much technically, but in order for us to understand him. And for all this, he is much more interesting, more present, and more relevant to us and our world.

There are many studies on the historical Jesus—some good, some bad. They have a laudable aim: to get back to the real Jesus. Looking at Jesus in his first-century context begins the adjustment of our mindset. It turns our focus on the man himself in his time. Of the various studies, N. T. Wright's *Jesus and the Victory of God* has had the greatest impact for me. Wright focuses with great intensity on Jesus' world, creating a fascinating portrait of the man himself. It feels as though the Jesus he introduces us to might just have been real.

It is worth dipping into some Wright.[1] He has an insatiable hope that we can get to Jesus through the Gospels. He trusts that the Gospel writers are doing more than propagating their own agenda. They actually get close to the real Jesus. Take what Wright says about Jesus' self-awareness and mission. If we want Jesus, we need to know what he thought about himself. To get to this, we need to understand him in relation to first-century people—their dreams, hopes, and fears. Wright observes that many Jews were hoping for a messiah—an anointed one from God who would restore their fortunes. What the messiah would look like varied from group to group. It is in this setting that Jesus figures out his vocation. He knew that a messiah would bring God's reign of justice, presence, and peace to his people and the whole earth. God's presence was meant to be in the temple, but the temple seemed empty. No wonder Zechariah was so surprised when an angel turned up there. The temple was meant to be God's blessing to the earth, but instead was sucking the life out of many through taxation. At the same time, it was excluding others altogether.

Jesus increasingly recognized that God's presence was not arriving through the temple but through himself. He was acting like the temple. His miracles, teachings, prophetic judgements—these were bringing in God's presence. That people sought him out just confirms this: lepers; prostitutes; the sick. They saw the love of God in him. They saw in him the God of the covenant, the God who had been victoriously present in the stories of their heritage. In Jesus, they knew they would find welcome, healing, and restoration. Jesus gets what is going on—gets somehow that God is running though his veins and out towards others. To put it in Wright's terms, Jesus sees that he is acting as the embodiment of the God of Israel.[2]

Jesus is not a heroic or mythic figure. Neither is he more God than human. He makes sense in this world and from the Scriptures. It makes at least some sense that a first-century Jew might understand his vocation as messianic considering what was taking place around him and through him. It also starts to make sense of early Christian claims about Jesus' divinity. Jesus acts and speaks in a way that brings the kingdom of God to bear on the world. He acts as Israel's God has been known to act. We can see why the Gospel writers highlight these aspects of Jesus' ministry. As they have pieced

---

1. On what follows, see Wright, *Jesus and the Victory*. In particular, chapters 9–10.

2. Wright summarizes this argument in "Jesus and the Identity of God."

accounts from various people together, they have been caught by who Jesus was. The Jesus they are narrating is who they believe him to be. They are compelled to talk about him. I am hooked on this Jesus. Why? Not least because he is luminous and real, but also because in him I see a God worthy of worship. I see something that relates not only to then, but to this moment.

So far, so interesting. But Wright is doing more than saying interesting stuff about Jesus. For him, when we read the gospels we are actually getting the first-century Jesus. This is significant because for a while modern scholarship had been brutally critical of the Gospel accounts. Actually, the criticisms haven't stopped.[3] People I speak to outside of Christianity with an awareness of the Gospels are suspicious of their authenticity, thinking they reflect the wishes of the authors rather than the real Jesus. Wright thinks such objections say more about the objectors than the gospels. Suspicion more likely reveals our own prejudices than exposing the truth. Rather than seeing the motives of the authors as sinister, it makes better sense to look at the Jesus they have been captivated by and the account they give of him.

Much as Wright's portrayal of Jesus is brilliant, I have some concerns. There is a tension. The tension is around approaching the Gospels objectively and being a Christian. I am not objective when it comes to Jesus. My feelings run too deep. I think Wright is trying to be objective when really it is not so important. I agree with him that the actual Jesus living in time and space is reachable. I too trust that the Gospel writers are talking about this Jesus. I agree that it is valuable to use historical tools to understand the context of the Gospels and so Jesus himself. But I also think that because the Gospel writers have faith in Jesus, their accounts display some of their allegiance to him. Their faith matters in relation to their portrayals. This is why I cannot just read the Gospels like history books, or even as biographies. I read them as a Christian. The faith bit—both our own and that of the Gospel writers—matters. When I come to these texts, it is as one who *wants* to believe in Jesus. My spectacles are rose-tinted. I would not have it any other way.

The Preexistent Jesus

Why does the faith bit matter? Some things to do with Jesus are more difficult to get at without faith. Take a theological concept such as Christ's preexistence. The Son lives eternally with Father and Spirit, existing before

3. See Wright's analysis of various views in *Jesus and the Victory*, 1–78.

taking human form as Jesus.[4] Swallowing a teaching like this is not easy. Because we are really not preexistent, we do not have a requisite framework for understanding preexistence. However good we are at history, we cannot get to Christ's preexistence by looking at the past. But it is a cornerstone of my belief. It is a belief that gives shape to everything else to do with Jesus. In Jesus, I see the eternal Son.

We can read about Christ's preexistence in the New Testament but that does not make it digestible or easy to understand. Take John 1:1: "In the beginning was the Word, and the Word was with God, and the Word was God." John's language, in particular, is deeply strange—otherworldly even. It is not like reading about Jesus' interactions with the disciples, for example. When we get to verse 14, "And the Word became flesh and lived among us, and we have seen his glory, the glory as of a father's only son," we are dealing with something within our world, though not wholly recognizable using our usual frameworks. The incarnation of the Word is incomprehensible as ordinary history. That does not mean that I treat it as myth, symbol, or mystery. I treat it as real—real in every sense. Nevertheless, I have to step into belief to see it as real. It takes an act of commitment.

We might say that grace is required for us to see Christ as the preexistent one. Many Christians have said something on these lines. We can only see what is true by grace. How I understand grace distinctively, though, is by tying it directly to the incarnation—to the movement of the eternal Son towards us. We can know the Son of God as the eternal one because he showed up amongst us—because he became flesh in the real world, our world, right before our eyes. The eternal Son literally moves towards us and opens our eyes. One author says, "Since the pre-existent reality of the eternal Son . . . actually became part of history, in return history bears the imprints of God's . . . reality."[5] We can know Jesus as the eternal Son in history, but we can only know because he became like us—only see because he acted towards, with, and in us. It is only in this divine and human act—this becoming flesh of the eternal Son—that our eyes are opened to his reality. That is the point; we cannot see Jesus as the eternal one unless we recognize him as such. It takes a step into the strange reality of the gospels to see and understand—to believe.

---

4. I use "before" here cautiously. Time and eternity are complex!

5. Deines, *Acts of God in History*, 414. Deines is summarizing the view of Martin Hengel.

The Son of God became human in our world. Nevertheless, we need the concept of Christ's preexistence to recognize him in fullness. He was God the eternal Son, the one who became flesh, but it requires more than dipping our feet into history to conclude this. It requires more of us than taking what the Bible says as historically true. Jesus is not just *a* truth accessible in the same way as other historical happenings. His reality is much more comprehensive than that. And to comprehend this reality we need grace and faith. Ultimately, we are required to step into believing in this Jesus. In this sense, my being Christian *is* dependent on grace. It is dependent on the becoming human of the divine Word. And it includes moving toward him in response to his moving toward us.

To show this more clearly, we can compare another way of understanding Christ from Scripture. Some would claim that Scripture is God's inspired and authoritative word that gets us straight to Jesus. Why make it more complex than that? When it says that Jesus was the Word, and the Word was God, we must just take it as truth. This is akin to saying that Jesus' preexistence is true because the Bible says it is true. We might call this a fundamentalist explanation. Why do I not say this? Because this reading can make the words of Scripture themselves the primary truth and Jesus the secondary truth. Granted, I don't expect many would say they believe Jesus is preexistent *only* because they believe Scripture is true. Nevertheless, in a desire to affirm the authority of Scripture there is a risk of making the words on the pages the center, rather than Christ. Jesus does not exist in the pages of Scripture. This is not a Christian claim. Jesus is not true *because* the Bible says he is true. Rather, Jesus is the living Son of God who has given himself to be known *through* Scripture as true.

This matters because when opening the Bible, I find I am not looking for inspired words; I am looking for a person. My concern is that this can come across as not evangelical. But I think it is. Evangelicalism is about the good news. Scripture talks about the good news but Scripture is only the good news because of what it refers to. I am interested in the account of Scripture because of *who* it is accounting for not because of the account itself. Jesus himself is the good news. He would be the good news even without Scripture. That said, the primary place we find Jesus *is* Scripture. But I also encounter this Jesus when I sing about him on a Sunday, when confessing he is Lord, when eating the bread, and drinking the cup. I feel something when doing these things. This in turn draws me back to

Scripture—to find him again—to sense the strength of testimony to him that the writers convey.

The passion of the Gospel writers is the living reality of Christ, not their own words. The reality of Christ is transformative of the world. Scripture faithfully tells us about this transformative reality, but is not the transformative agent itself. When we come to recognize the nature of Scripture in terms of its being a book of the church, a document of faith through commitment, a testament to the truth, we cannot see it anymore as a document true in isolation. If it is true, it is true in relation to its object, true in relation to the thing itself, true despite itself. It is true *for* the world, not just for truth's sake. For many, this argument is a foregone conclusion. For others, what I am saying might be unacceptable. Hopefully, though, for some at least, there is something here that makes sense and does due honor to Christ *and* Scripture.

Positively, I am claiming that the Bible is authoritative because the Word became flesh. This is not an easy claim. As said, it requires faith and allegiance to end up here.[6] The nub of the claim is not open to historical enquiry in any ordinary sense. I can never lose sight of the fact that when approaching the text, I do so as a Christian passionate about the person we find in its pages. When I read the gospels, I do so as one captivated by the eternal Christ, not just through intellectual ascent, but also in terms of my motivation and commitment. To keep rational integrity, I must admit my passion for the content of Christian witness. Only then can its content be understood as true—as meaningful. A note here from C. S. Lewis might be of help. Talking of the gospels and his own movement towards Christianity, he states:

> I was by now too experienced in literary criticism to regard the Gospels as myths. They had not the mythical taste. And yet the very matter which they set down in their artless, *historical* fashion . . . was precisely the matter of the great myths. If ever a myth had become *fact*, had been incarnated, it would be just like this . . . Here and here only in all time the myth must have become fact; the Word, flesh; God, Man. This is not "a religion," nor "a philosophy." It is the summing up and actuality of them all.[7]

6. Recent interpretation on Paul suggests that faith "pistis" should be seen as "allegiance" rather than "rational ascent." Without getting into the details, I think both terms are useful. See Bates, *Salvation by Allegiance Alone*, 4 and throughout.

7. Quoted in Art Lindsley, "Importance of Imagination," 2. Italics mine.

Whether we come from doubt or from belief (Lewis came from doubt), the validation of the Gospels is the reality they refer to, and this reality is one that has stepped towards us. I still want to be a Christian because of the Jesus who reaches out from Scripture. If he is real, I cannot turn aside. I must run towards him, not away from him.

I confess with Christians through the ages, that Jesus is God incarnate, that he reveals the reality of God and that his life, death and resurrection are game-changing real events. I not only believe these things; my life is shaped around them; they have imminent meaning. Admitting my frame of reference does not make what I am talking about objectively true or false, but if we do not admit our bias, we place a load on the Bible it is not meant to bear. Approaching the Bible with complete objectivity is both impossible and undesirable. If we are Christian, we are more likely to allow the Bible to have authority in our lives. We need not shy away from this. We needn't pretend we do not have this Christian worldview we bring to the text. Ultimately, my being Christian is not motivated by belief in the absolutely trustworthiness of Scripture. I am Christian because of the movement of the eternal Word towards humanity in Jesus.

Many will not see my argument as controversial. The point is not to be contentious. However, I disagree with a certain form of fundamentalism that in its insistence on the absolute authority of Scripture ends up making a claim over and above Scripture. Fundamentalism does not just have a problematic view of Scripture; it fails to recognize the problem of the self in approaching the text. It doesn't listen well enough to some key thinkers of Christian history: Augustine, Luther, Calvin, etc. They saw sin as a reason why we cannot approach the text in perfect purity.[8] Our ability to see is flawed. Theological honesty is so important because when we admit our biases, including our sinful view of the world, we recognize both our need of the Spirit and others to help us in our weakness. We become more likely to be accountable to fellow interpreters in the Christian community past and present. We allow others to shape our reading of Scripture. I have realized increasingly that it is no good agreeing with an exciting interpretation of a passage that no one else agrees with. It is probably exciting because it confirms something I already believed. If this reading only works for me, then I am likely just reading into the text what I want to see. If I allow this reading to become authoritative, then the fact that I am a flawed interpreter is missed.

---

8. It doesn't follow that my approach to Scripture is the same as theirs.

One might object that I am being too negative about human nature or too blinkered by my own shortcomings. But if my ability to see is flawed, so is the ability of others. Maybe I should be more hopeful of accessing the meaning of the biblical text objectively despite my flaws. Perhaps with the help of the Spirit we can get through to the truth of the text. However, we see from Christian history that an agreed objective reading is nowhere to be found. Despite wide acknowledgement of the authority of Scripture, serious disagreements exist regarding its meaning and application. We don't get around this by getting to some kind of unbiased reading. Rather, we deal with it by being open about our stories, our biases, and by working them through with others—ideally, others different to ourselves.

In my church, we recently completed a mid-week bible study focusing on diversity through the book of Acts.[9] We shared our stories of difference: socioeconomic, cultural, ethnic, educational, etc. Sharing stories helps us see what we bring to the text. It serves to highlight our cultural blind spots. As we opened the Bible together, we saw something new. We started to see through the eyes of others. The stories of some included real adversity, including discrimination. Others talked simply of feeling like a square peg in a round hole. Everyone recognized that what they bring to their faith, in terms of experience, matters. Hearing such stories means we come away changed, with our assumptions unsettled. We don't reach this place when we read Scripture in a vacuum—in isolation. Reading Scripture in a diverse community connects us to the world of the Bible—connects us to a world that looks different to our own. The connection is possible, but not in a bubble.

We have every reason to be hopeful when we read the Bible. The one we seek in its pages is not elusive. In fact, the Jesus of Scripture is luminous. Reading about him is an emotional and personal experience. It relates to worship as much as it relates to study. As the worshiping community— the community that seeks after this same Jesus—we can be positive about working together to encounter him in the present. Indeed, the community of readers, those who gather to read about Jesus, are another part of my continuing desire to be Christian. I have been in the room with people of diverse backgrounds, ages, and experiences. Through dialogue and prayer, we have found the Christ of Scripture. When such a diverse community comes together to seek him, there is reason to be hopeful and joyful.

9. We used the "INVITED" series produced by King Church London. See https://kingschurchlondon.org/invited/.

Jesus and the Old Testament

Some find Christ all over the place in the Old Testament: in prophecy, ritu-
al, and preincarnate appearances. The beauty of this view is the high value
it places on God's eternal Triunity and providence. God's sovereign hand
is at work leading to Christ as the fulfillment of the divine purpose. Seeing
Christ as the fulfillment of Old Testament prophecy also appears to prove
the Bible right. I agreed with this view until one of my lecturers suggested
that the Old Testament passages did *not* have Jesus Christ as we know him
in mind. They are not predicting the Word incarnate who is to come—not
in any straightforward way at least. So what of the New Testament's use of
the Old Testament regarding Christ? Does this not imply that the prophets of old had him view? The New Testament reference is legitimate, we
heard, because the Spirit is enabling fresh interpretation.[10] At the time, my
response was that at least some passages were prophesying Christ. Surely
Isaiah 7:14, for example, was about him: "Therefore the Lord himself will
give you a sign. Look, the young woman is with child and shall bear a son,
and shall name him Immanuel." However, even on a passage such as this,
my view changed.

I would hear something taught like "Jesus was the guy in the fire with
Shadrach, Meshach, and Abednego" and think, "ah yes." Well was he? Does
the story not lose something of its immediate meaning if we jump to saying
it was the preincarnate Christ in there? Richard Hays suggests that rather
than seeing Old Testament passages as predictive or self-fulfilling we might
see them as "pre-figural."[11] Such passages prefigure what we find in Jesus in
a meaningful way—but not directly; not predictively. Jesus embraces these
texts in his ministry and self-understanding, but this does not mean they
are about him as such. Yes, he fulfills the longing of the prophets; yes, he
is the fulfillment of God's work amongst his people, but this is an unprecedented fact until he comes in the flesh. The texts themselves do not fully
anticipate what will come.

This liberates my reading of both the New and Old Testaments. The
Old Testament regains its ability to speak into the moment; the New Testa-
ment gives fresh voice to the prophets as we see their words in the light of
Christ. I am happy to say that when we read the Old Testament, we see how
God's plan with the world always had Christ as its intention. However, it is

10. The lecturer was the late Gordon Thomas.
11. See particularly the introduction to Hays, *Reading Backwards*, 1–16.

in knowing Christ, particularly through the testimony of the New Testament, that we are enabled to read the Old Testament in this fresh way.

Why focus on this problem? Because of the implications for understanding both Christ and Scripture. Anything that prioritizes the watertightness of the Bible over and above its chief character, is unconvincing. As soon as we try to prove the trustworthiness of Scripture, we are on shaky ground. If the main significance of the Old Testament is that it is proven right by the coming of Christ, it then loses its relevance to the world into which it speaks. Scripture is not primarily a self-certifying document. It speaks outwards rather than inwards. That is its dramatic and prophetic power. This does not mean that Jesus has nothing to do with the Old Testament. Indeed, he perfects the hope to which it points. The inbreaking of the Word made flesh in the first century is a unique and unprecedented reality. Scripture catches this reality rather than produces it.

In summary, I treat Scripture as inspired and wholly authoritative, but the conditions for its authority do not lie in its own structure. Its authority lies in its object of reference—in the Christ who the New Testament authors consider the Old Testament to have prefigured. This does not mean Scripture is never self-certifying, but if it is *only* self-certifying, it never reaches the flesh and blood of Jesus, let alone his divinity. Scripture is not Jesus. By this, I mean that although Scripture is inspired, it is not the Word himself. The Bible is the prime testimony to the Word; its testimony is in every way enough, but we shouldn't make it do more than its human authors can bear. The deep and beautiful truth of Christian proclamation is God's revelation in Christ himself. Spoken of in Scripture—yes. Testified to in Scripture— yes. Wholly contained in Scripture—no. Scripture's authority is externally validated not by historical research, not even by faith, but by its object.

What I have said here does not result in a low view of Scripture— quite the reverse. Scripture has a revitalized place. It becomes dynamic. It becomes imminent. It has a fresher prophetic edge. It leaves things more open, less resolved, more pregnant. Thus, Scripture also relates to my present Christian existence. I see in this book the hope and promise of Jesus Christ. I want to read it every day because of what it promises. The Bible speaks directly into the world—my world. As Scripture testifies to a transformative vision of a moment past, so it speaks to the transformative moment of now.

2

Christt the Son

From Scripture to Christ

FOR THE EARLY CHURCH, figuring out the nature of Christ was everything. In particular, establishing whether he was divine, human, or both. Getting to grips with this discussion whilst in college left an indelible impression on me. The Nicene Creed offers an authoritative word on the matter. Within this ancient creed, we find an astonishing description of Christ. Of all the things said, the most striking is Christ being of "one being" (Gr. *homoousion*) with the Father. The man Jesus is no less than God:

> We believe in one Lord, Jesus Christ,
> the only Son of God,
> eternally begotten of the Father,
> God from God, Light from Light,
> true God from true God,
> begotten, not made,
> of one Being with the Father;
> through him all things were made.
> For us and for our salvation
> he came down from heaven,
> was incarnate of the Holy Spirit and the Virgin Mary
> and became truly human.[1]

The power of this teaching that Jesus was of the same stuff as God the Father never loses its impact, however much I reflect on it. It is the central pillar of my faith. When we talk about the man Jesus, we are talking about the same Son who is eternally equal in divinity with the Father. Jesus is not

---

1. Lines 5–16, retrieved from https://www.ucc.org/beliefs_nicene-creed.

a lesser being than God, not a representation of God, not a pointer towards God; no, Jesus is God. He is also human. He does not cheat at being human; he is not part human—he is fully human. Anything valid that we might say of divinity, we can say of Jesus; anything valid we say about being human, we can say of Jesus. In Jesus, divinity and humanity are drawn together. As the creed says, the one who is "true God" "became truly human." And this "for our salvation." Jesus' divinity and humanity are not just to do with him; they are to do with us. Something is happening for us when the divine Son assumes human flesh. The incarnation is not just remarkable in itself; it is remarkable for what it brings about.

But it is not self-evident how we get from the Scriptures to a belief in the full divinity and humanity of Christ. We can believe what the Bible says; we can even give an account of how the early Christians came to worship Jesus as God; but none of this quite prepares us for recognizing him as this one. I have spoken about some problems related to Scripture. I now offer a way forward. What I am interested in is moving from reading Scripture to recognizing Jesus as God *now*. This is no less than a question of how we get from human words to encountering God himself in the Son. It is working out how Jesus, who is himself God, can be *known* to be. If Christ is not the divine and human one, then my faith falls down. Not because it puts everything believed in at stake, but if divinity has not become humanity in him, then there is no hope for humanity. We humans need the incarnation. Without it, we are in the dark. With it, we come into the light. This sounds dramatic, and it is.

Maybe our best hope of grasping the divinity of Christ comes not first from the biblical text, but from the reality of his becoming human itself. Jesus bridges the gap between divine and human. Scripture then comes in as a testimony to that reality. Christ is therefore the key to Scripture. The same gap that exists between human and divine exists between us and what the text of Scripture testifies to. Alan Torrance puts this in terms of being able to proceed from *reading* about the Son of God to actually *knowing* him as God.[2] The human words of Scripture can testify to Christ the Son because of the reconciliation that has taken place between humanity and God in Christ's incarnation. Because Jesus is of one being with the Father, so humanity is reconciled with God and so our human words—Scripture— display this reconciliation, particularly as they refer to this reconciling one himself. This is a lot to digest. It is almost as difficult to digest as the

2. See Torrance, "Can the Truth Be Learned?," 143–65.

Christian gospel itself. But to put it as simply as possible, Scripture is possible because the gift of salvation has come to us.

I speak to people who insist there must be human error in Scripture. That is what our experience of being human tells us. We make mistakes; or worse, we intentionally mislead. What they don't see is that Christ's incarnation is the taking hold of human speech to redeem it. It is another grace thing. Just as God's coming into the world is an act of grace, so Scripture authoritatively testifying to this divine act is grace. How do we know that Scripture is God's authoritative word? Because of the work of Christ in reconciling humanity with God; because of what Christ has done for the human situation; because the gap has been bridged.

The great value in such an understanding is not only what it means for Scripture but also our reception of Scripture. Because we are fallen, limited, errant, fallible, and all the rest, we need God's grace. We often recognize our dependence on God's grace for our salvation, but we don't always extend the same need for grace to our reading of Scripture. I think we must. We do not receive saving grace from Scripture; we receive it from Jesus. We receive it because God has moved towards us in Christ. So with Scripture. Scripture reading in the community—the church—is possible because this same community acknowledges that Christ has bridged the gap. We read as the redeemed community. We can have every hope, therefore, that when we read, we are getting Jesus, just as we can have every hope he has done everything for our salvation. I read Scripture not because it is the inerrant, infallible word of God, but because of who I am reading about. I choose to trust the Bible just as I trust the one of whom it speaks. And find I can— find I want to—because of what I read.

Karl Barth

When I was nineteen years old, I moved into an inner-city estate in Manchester with a group of other Christians as part of a youth work project. The estate had all the problems you could imagine: gang culture, drug culture, gun crime, knife crime, etc. Not everything was bleak. There was plenty of love on offer in the shape of family loyalty and protection, but the brokenness was deep. After a few years living there, I started at theological college as a mature student. A selection of Barth's *Church Dogmatics* was required reading. I lapped it up.[3] Barth's theology spoke in dynamic terms to the dra-

---

3. Gollwitzer, *Dogmatics in Outline*.

matic events of his day. He saw like few others the problems with so-called enlightened Europe as it crashed into the first World War. Likewise, he looked out on a Germany shattered by war and saw a barren wasteland. Out of that wasteland, the Third Reich would eventually come to power. He directed his gaze at the Führer, and boldly stated that the Führer was not his God—only Jesus Christ, revealed in Scripture. He rallied together those who would confess his name. He found the surrounding evil around him unexplainable without recovering the guts of the gospel—the extent of our sinfulness, and our absolute need of God's coming in Christ. And he didn't point the finger. He, as much as anyone, recognized Paul's words, "all have sinned and fall short of the glory of God."[4]

Barth's emphatic insistence on the incapacity of us humans to comprehend God on our own terms spoke right to me. Barth laid bare the brokenness I found in the human condition, both in myself and those around me. Sin—particularly the sin of a society that enables such deprivation—was all too clear. There is something wrong with the human situation. Things are not as they should be, including our ability to comprehend God. Acknowledging the full extent of the brokenness of the human condition means theology cannot be built on "reason," "nature," or even "experience" (despite what I have said about experience). These things depend too much on my goodness. I cannot depend on my goodness or the goodness of others. We *can*, however, depend upon God's desire to be known in Jesus Christ, upon how God gives himself to be known.

It is ordinary for Christians to say that Christ is the revelation of God. However, we can be very particular about this. If we want to know who God is, it is at Jesus we must look. Without Jesus, we cannot say anything of worth about God. This is something Barth is emphatic about. Reading Barth has formed much of my theology, not least in the areas so far discussed. We can now give attention to some of his insights.

We can only understand God in his self-revelation. For Barth, this revelation comes through Jesus, testified to in Scripture. Thus:

> If . . . we ask further concerning the one point upon which, according to Scripture, our attention and thoughts should and must be concentrated, then from first to last the Bible directs us to the name of Jesus Christ. It is in this name that we discern the divine

---

4. Rom 3:23. Barth's unfaithfulness is a difficult thing to come to terms with. Others have told of how this might discredit his theology. See, for example, Galli, "What to Make of Barth's Steadfast Adultery."

decision in favour of the movement towards this people, the self-determination of God as Lord and shepherd of this people.[5]

For Barth there can be no way of knowing God outside of Jesus Christ. And we can only understand Jesus Christ because he has come to us. In reading Scripture, we get to witness his coming. In fact, we are caught up in the event of his coming.

Some criticize Barth for overemphasizing Christology whilst underemphasizing where else we might find God. In Barth's Christianity, says Dietrich Bonhoeffer, one must swallow everything to do with Christ—incarnation, divinity, resurrection—to be properly Christian. It is a like it or lump it thing.[6] Bonhoeffer might be right about Barth. But this is the Christianity that pulls me in. If I were to look anywhere other than Jesus, I would no longer be Christian. The intention is not to dictate the terms of Christianity, more explain the state of affairs for myself. In Jesus, I find the way, the truth, and the life. This is the version of Christianity that decides to trust what Scripture says about Jesus. It believes that this same Jesus, in very nature God, took our form and thus enabled us to comprehend God. Even as the words of Scripture are born out of a human hand, they are graciously enabled to testify to the truth. For me, this Christianity is not absolutist and closed, but humbly held, acknowledging the complexities involved. It is a matter of trust. In accepting Christ as the way, I do so whilst acknowledging what a gift that is.

In being insistent on Jesus as God's revelation, Barth criticizes the place of experience. Experience is not a reliable guide. Experience does not reveal God. But can we not both affirm experience *and* see Jesus as the full revelation of God? I think so. Barth has important reasons for his criticisms. By experience, he means something particular. He is responding to the liberal theology of his teachers, particularly those influenced by Friedrich Schleiermacher. Schleiermacher is considered the father of liberal theology. For him, self-consciousness or "feeling" is what makes up Christian faith. Being Christian "feels" like something. Barth pushes back, saying that true revelation is not a "sense," not based on feeling; it is based on something real. It is based on God's self-revelation in Jesus Christ. Revelation comes from God's side, not our side. God's revelation in Christ is real whether

---

5. Barth, *CD* 2/2.53.
6. Bonhoeffer, *Letter's and Papers*, 286.

we feel it or not. God's revelation may capture our feelings but our feelings have nothing to do with it as such.[7]

I agree with much in Barth here. But I also think that feeling—or experience—*is* part of what it means to be Christian. At least, it is part of my being Christian. It is worth clarifying, therefore, what is and what is not being said about experience. Schleiermacher sees true faith as absolute dependency on God. To be Christian is to depend on God. I agree. But for Schleiermacher, what we can know of God relates directly to this absolute dependency.[8] He ties knowledge and dependency so tightly that he is left in a difficult place when confronted by God's revelation in Christ. For Barth, it is not because of our dependency on God that we have knowledge, but because of God's act towards us. Here I'm with Barth. It is not the "feeling" that makes me Christian, but God's gift in the Son. Yes, we can feel what it means to be Christian because of what God has done in Christ. But this requires him being the revelation of God. It requires his incarnation. Wrapped up in my feelings for God is the fact that in Jesus I see something real. I have these feelings because who he is and what he has done actually has a bearing on me.

Christ, for Schleiermacher, is not the actual conjunction of divine and human natures—he is not of one being with the Father. He is merely the ideal version of one who absolutely depends on God. Only on this basis is he the one who facilitates the human/divine possibility. Schleiermacher can even say that Christ's humanity is redemptive for our humanity, but this does not make him God incarnate.[9] Also, whether Jesus is who the Gospels say he is, is not so important for Schleiermacher. For him, our Christian faith, our dependency on God, is not dependent on whether Jesus of Nazareth walked the earth in the way the Gospels say he did.

It will be seen from what has been said that I cannot accept what Schleiermacher says here. It amounts to reducing Christ to a human ideal, or even a divine ideal. To me, it matters that he is who Scripture says he is. So why bother with Schleiermacher? Because he offers a theology that starts with the experience of the Christian. My experience of the Christian faith, when at its best, looks like absolute dependency on God. And this relates to feeling. Feeling matters. To that extent, I agree with Schleiermacher. What happens in the experience of the Christian—my experience—however

---

7. See, McCormack, "What Has Basel to Do with Berlin," 81–82.

8. See, for example, Schleiermacher, *The Christian Faith*, 26.

9. Schleiermacher, *The Christian Faith*, 81–83.

indulgent that sounds, is key to understanding the God who reveals himself in Christ. But I don't want to be misunderstood in saying this. I don't want it to appear as though the truth of the gospel is dependent on my feelings.

I agree with Barth that we should base Christian faith on something given, not on something internal, but this does not mean that feelings have no place. We must focus knowledge of God on Christ—the Word of God incarnate—but we don't have to separate experience from revelation. Indeed, I have shown that our experience makes *more* sense when grounded in the objective basis of revelation—Jesus Christ. This may not be satisfactory for Barth, but it is the way in which I want to reconcile feelings with God's revelation in Christ.

To stick with Barth for a moment, we may revisit our discussion of Old and New Testaments. This will help highlight why I find Barth's theological vision so compelling. He follows the basic pattern we have already seen whereby "the New Testament is concealed within the Old, and the Old Testament is revealed by the New."[10] But what is of particular importance to him is that Christ's incarnation is always in view for God. For Barth, there is only one covenant, and this covenant is Christ himself. This is the covenant spoken about in the Hebrew Scriptures and fulfilled in Christ's coming. God's intended way of dealing with humanity was always to be Christ and will always be. To agree with Barth here is not to go back on saying the Hebrew Scriptures are pre-figural as opposed to direct in their testimony to Christ. It is to say that the goal of God's dealings with his people Israel is wrapped up in Christ.

Barth's centering on Christ speaks of God's loving intention for his people. The New Testament is fulfillment in the sense that the meaning of the covenant is disclosed in this person Jesus. But Barth is not saying that the Old Testament texts give us Christ, or predict Christ. We need to see Christ first to see him as the fulfillment of the covenant. Of the New Testament witness, Barth says, "What these men saw and heard, what their hands touched, was the fulfillment of the covenant in the existence and appearance of the one human partner who was obedient to God."[11] God intends the incarnation eternally. And this is where it becomes significant for me. Christ is not given as a fallback plan when creation goes wrong. Christ is not *just* a substitute for us in our failings. Rather, Christ is God's

---

10. Barth, *Evangelical Theology*, 28.
11. Barth, *Evangelical Theology*, 28.

original intention for his people. Christ is God's way of being with us and for us. Christ is in every sense God's word of love for us for all time.

In the view of some, there is an ugly elephant in Karl Barth's room. They cannot accept his theology because he does not contend for biblical inerrancy—the belief that Scripture is wholly without errors. Evangelicalism historically insists on inerrancy. A theologian like Wayne Grudem, at one time popular in my tradition,[12] is emphatic about this. He poses the following problem: "If Inerrancy is Denied, We Begin to Wonder If We Can Really Trust God in Anything He Says."[13] Who God is, how he speaks into the world, is so wrapped up in the words of Scripture—what amount to Grudem as essentially God's words—that were we to question inerrancy, everything else would fall to pieces. Theology then becomes something that fulfills the principle of inerrancy. Inerrancy confirms theology and theology confirms inerrancy. Texts become proof texts; absolute truths, true in themselves regardless of their referent. Grudem might not accept that last point, but the implication is there.

Barth's fear is that we could make the principle of inerrancy higher than the content of the text—higher than what the text is referring to. We would then get blanket support for making the text say whatever we want it to because it is God's word. We are not the master interpreters, says Barth; we are mere servants of the word.[14] Regardless of whether one agrees with Barth, I would at least want to say that inerrancy should not be the starting point for reading the Bible. Saying this does not amount to a denial of inerrancy, but is an acknowledgement that the object of faith is not the principle of inerrancy. I see Scripture as inspired, unique, and authoritative. But inerrancy is not central to my Christian belief. Barth's rejection of the principle is certainly understandable and not a reason to reject his whole theology. Evangelicals can read and learn from Barth without feeling guilty! Even in his denial of inerrancy, he can teach us something. He can teach us that the beauty of Scripture does not come from the accuracy of the words, or whether it stands up against science. What matters is its message and its referent.

12. And still with some.

13. Grudem, *Systematic Theology*, 100.

14. Barth makes the same point about human speech in relation to Christ: "We are unprofitable servants, and in no sense are we to imagine that we have become in the very least masters of the subject." Barth, *CD* 1/1.83.

A further objection to Barth is worth considering before we move on. Some evangelicals accuse him of seeing Scripture as authoritative only in the moment of encounter—as we read it. There is something going on when we read—an event of revelation. The understandable concern here is that if Scripture only becomes true in this encounter, then it calls into question whether it is true in itself. When I read Barth, however, particularly in his later writing, I see a deep trust in Scripture. And it is not just a trust in its message; it is a trust in the actual content and the reality it purports to. He builds his work on the Bible.

Again, we miss something if we don't hear what he is saying. There is something going on when we read Scripture. An encounter *is* taking place. We are being transformed, renewed, and joined to the truth. When reading Scripture, I want to be ready to change, not just have preheld thoughts confirmed. This does not mean that the text has no authority of its own. It does. I do not agree with everything Barth says on the matter. His account of what Scripture is in and of itself is not wholly convincing. Does Scripture itself offer us its object regardless of whether it transforms us in the process? I would say yes. I want to say more for Scripture itself, both for its historical trustworthiness and for its completeness. But I also want to contend for what Barth is saying—to contend for an approach to Scripture whereby the Christ testified to, is the Christ who enables our transformation as readers; as we read, we encounter something for the moment. I for one need this encounter and this transformation.

Christ for Us

We need to get back to Christ himself. Who is Christ *for us*? I have always thought of Jesus in terms of his relationship with people—even people like me. The incarnation says that his being in the flesh has something to do with us. The Gospels show him being with people and for people. Just as he was for them, so he is for us. Just as he loved them, so he loves us. This claim is fuel for the philosopher's fire: of course we want to think Jesus loves us. We are likely to hold on to this belief at all costs. The philosopher, or the psychologist, would say that we are projecting our wishes on to Jesus. But the love we see in Jesus is not dreamy, romantic, or sentimentalist. It would be difficult to read the Gospels and conclude that Jesus fulfills any of the aforementioned adjectives. He is not presented as an easy figure. The love he displays is costly, radical, and challenging. This stops it *only* being about fulfilling my wishes. In fact, his love for us is not something easy to bear. His love unsettles notions of love we had before. It is a love that demands that my life is now different.

Whilst in prison, Dietrich Bonhoeffer asks a burning question: "Who is Jesus Christ for us today?"[15] For him, "who" Christ is, is more important than "how" he can be that person. Who he is for us "today" pushes us to think about how his life impinges upon ours now—in this moment. He is challenging us to think what we are about in relation to this Jesus. And who is Jesus for us in the present? Yes, Jesus is the incarnation of the Word; he is of the same being as the Father; he is also fully human. I see him as all these things. But how does that relate to us now? It is an important question because if he is for us, that has to mean something; it has to give birth to something.

What does it mean that Christ is for us today? We will come back to the immanency of the question shortly. First, we can look at another implication of Christ's being for us. Christ's being for humanity means also that God is for humanity. Kathryn Tanner expresses it thus:

> Christ epitomizes in supreme form God's overall intent with respect to us; and thereby gives that intent a concrete shape we can follow. The whole of who God is for us as creator and redeemer, which in its varied complexity might simply overwhelm and mystify us, is found in concentrated compass in Christ.[16]

Who Christ is for us, is who God is for us. We can flip the point. What does it look like for God to be for us? It looks like Jesus Christ. Christ is the shape of God's being for us. Here in Christ, we find God for us. There are implications for the nature of God here that we will return to in the final part. But for now, we can affirm that all we say about Christ, from his eternal nature, to the way he is with people in the Gospels, we can say about God.

In one sense, I am just expressing a central element of orthodoxy. In another, I am highlighting something others have missed, or have not allowed to take full force. Some popular construals of Reformed evangelicalism, for example, place plenty of emphasis on Christ, but more for his work in bringing about salvation, more for what he does in obedience to the Father, more for how what he does enables the Father to be glorified. For instance, John Piper insists that "When the universality of things was

---

15. Bonhoeffer, "Lectures on Christology," 299–360.
16. Tanner, *Christ the Key*, viii.

considered, the death of the Son of God was seen by the Father as a magnificent way to demonstrate His righteousness."[17] The work of Christ here is for the sake of the Father's righteousness. I am sure this is true, but it suggests that the Father is still the hierarchically important one, and that Christ is merely the facilitator of the Father's work. This will not do. Christ is rather the one who is the reality of God for us; the one in whom we are to look to if we want to see who and how God is. He is the center of God's being for us.[18]

The meaning of Christ's reality for us relates to our "today"—our "now." And here we can talk once more about our experience. I need to shoot from the hip for a moment. For me, the appeal of Christianity does not lie in rational argument—that much should be obvious by now. It is more embodied than that. Objective arguments often have nothing to do with *us*. Jesus Christ, however, has everything to do with us. The Christian faith I am interested in has something to do with the wholeness of life. That is why the "now" question is so important. Because when we look at Jesus as he is, it challenges us to think who we are in relation to him in the moment. And it becomes an ongoing thing; it becomes, "what will my life look like in relation to his being for me?" That is why I cannot approach Jesus disinterestedly: both because of who he is and because of who I am in relation to him.

My motivations relate to his being for us. My humanity relates to his humanity and he in turn relates humanity to his divinity. His divinity means we are talking about the reality of God. It is not just about me; it is about God. Likewise, his humanity means it is not just about me. It is about everyone, because Christ's being human relates to everyone. Jesus takes a particular humanity, but in assuming it he represents the whole of humanity, then and now. His assuming of one humanity is done for the sake of all. My "now," therefore, relates to the "now" of everyone I encounter, because we have in common the fact that Jesus exists for us—that God exists for us. What this means for me today is not just a belief; it is a commitment and a practice. His reality rubs off on me. Because Jesus is for us, I must be for others. When I am not, I contradict Christ's divine and human work.

We can now draw a few threads together. It will be clear that I do not think that Christ only exists as a principle or in my experience. This applies to saying he exists "for us" as much as it does to anything else. The

17. Piper, *Desiring God*, 40.
18. It is not that Piper would disagree, but it is a matter of emphasis.

Christ who is the object of my desire, to return to where we started, is the biblical and historical Christ. He is real. The actual entering into time of Christ as the incarnate Word bit is critical. We cannot prove the biblical accounts of Jesus are historically accurate, particularly accounts of his pre-existence, but I treat them as historical—as true. The divine Son embraced a particular existence on this earth as human. But reading the accounts of Jesus as historical is a theological claim itself, because by accepting these accounts I likewise accept, for example, Christ's preexistence. In doing so, I accept—embrace—that from all eternity, Christ entered the world for us. This is challenging. It not only requires faith, allegiance and commitment; it also requires that I see the world differently. It means I must likewise exist for others. My action must flow from Christ himself. When I talk about wanting to be a Christian, I am talking about a faith commitment worked out in relation to the world. Seeing Christ as he is gives me the desire and motivation to live for others. This is evangelical because it is emphatically good news. Christ being for us; God being for us; is good news. It is news worth sharing, both because it is good and because it relates to all. Christ's being for me means also Christ being for everyone and his being for everyone is something to be happy about.

We now zoom in on a Gospel narrative rather than continuing to talk about Christ at a distance. Through a sermon, we enter the Garden of Gethsemane to see how what has been said takes expression.

3

Gethsemane

A Sermon

Matthew 26:36–46

36Then Jesus went with them to a place called Gethsemane; and he said to his disciples, "Sit here while I go over there and pray." 37He took with him Peter and the two sons of Zebedee, and began to be grieved and agitated. 38Then he said to them, "I am deeply grieved, even to death; remain here, and stay awake with me." 39And going a little farther, he threw himself on the ground and prayed, "My Father, if it is possible, let this cup pass from me; yet not what I want but what you want." 40Then he came to the disciples and found them sleeping; and he said to Peter, "So, could you not stay awake with me one hour? 41Stay awake and pray that you may not come into the time of trial; the spirit indeed is willing, but the flesh is weak." 42Again he went away for the second time and prayed, "My Father, if this cannot pass unless I drink it, your will be done." 43Again he came and found them sleeping, for their eyes were heavy. 44So leaving them again, he went away and prayed for the third time, saying the same words. 45Then he came to the disciples and said to them, "Are you still sleeping and taking your rest? See, the hour is at hand, and the Son of Man is betrayed into the hands of sinners. 46Get up, let us be going. See, my betrayer is at hand."

AS A CHILD, I sang a solo in a Good Friday school assembly. I can no longer find the words, but it was written from the perspective of Jesus in Gethsemane. Here was expressed Christ's inner turmoil: his questioning;

his anxiety. The lyrics profoundly moved me even then. I have always been gripped by Gethsemane. At the very least, Jesus' words are emotional and thought-provoking, at most, deeply unsettling. They raise serious questions: Is he having second thoughts? Are the will of the Son and his Father somehow at odds? Does Jesus know what is going to happen—where this will ultimately lead? When we ponder this passage and these questions, we can be a mixed bag of thoughts and emotions. We bring certain experiences to bear. We come with a view of who Christ is. The way I see him provides a lens through which I see the story. I am a biased observer. When I see Jesus enter the garden, I do so believing he is not just another would-be religious leader. He enters as the Word become flesh for our sakes, as the incarnation of the Son of God. I also see his entering the garden as a real event.

There is something about this story that speaks to our experience. We might not think we have experienced anything like Gethsemane—how could we have done? But we all have emotional struggles. We have invariably experienced doubt and distress. I increasingly realize that I know little about what is going on in most people's lives. But with those I do get to know well, it more often than not becomes apparent that they have faced acutely distressing circumstances at some stage. Some of us might be in distress today.

But first, Gethsemane is really about Christ's agony. Yes, it speaks to human pain, and therefore into human experience. But we need to know how things lie with the lead character before thinking about ourselves. It is notable that Jesus wants the disciples to observe the events unfolding. In one sense, they are just bystanders—at least to begin with. But their presence is not coincidental. In particular, Jesus takes with him Peter and the two sons of Zebedee, James and John (v. 37). He asks them to stay close by—about a stone's throw away—whilst he goes a little further. The disciples have been following Jesus for a few years now. It has been an emotional rollercoaster—a whirlwind that has not let up for a moment. They have left everything to follow Jesus and have seen him do amazing wonders. But of late, he has been saying puzzling things about having to suffer and die. They are beyond the point of feeling tired. Now they are on complete shut-down mode. But Jesus asks them to stay awake. They fail, presumably because of the extent of their distress.

Although not right next to Jesus when he is praying, they must know what he is doing (otherwise we wouldn't have the account!). They see some of his distress. He has invited them to see. Jesus invites us too to observe this dark moment of his. But he does not demand our support. It would be too much for us—just as it was too much for the disciples. This is why he doesn't chastise them too much when they cannot stay awake. Likewise, he doesn't primarily invite the disciples to Gethsemane for them to realize what a cost *they* will have to pay—that will come later.

Although the disciples are present, Jesus goes it alone. Verse 39 says he goes "a little farther" in order to pray. The full extent of emotional distress is born by him only. The disciples are protected by their ability to sleep through it. Sleep can be a protection—a gift. Sometimes we don't value it enough. What is the significance of Jesus going alone? He goes alone because he doesn't want the disciples to take the burden themselves—not the full weight of it. We, likewise, are not called to take the whole weight of Christ's work. We wouldn't be able to. Jesus knows something horrific is in store for him and how difficult it would be for his friends if they came all the way with him. Following Jesus is not going to get easier anytime soon.

Jesus knows what is coming, not from some kind of divine mindset present in him, but because he knows that what he has been teaching and doing—wrangling with law makers; forgiving sinners; all the rest of it—has been unacceptable to so many, blasphemous to some. He is too much of an agitator to stay alive. The clash of Jesus with historical powers is enough to make his crucifixion likely. We lose something of the reality of the cross if we theologize it too quickly. Even the disciples might have worked out something like this would happen if they had dared think about it, even without the hints Jesus had given them.

Jesus knows he is going to his death, but even though he asks us to take up our crosses, we are not going to this same death. In his death he takes responsibility for us; he takes our burdens. He realizes that because of how God is using him—through word, deed, and symbol—he has this vocation as the divine Son that will cost him his life. What he is doing is not just identifying with us; he is acting *for us*; doing what we cannot. Even Gethsemane, therefore, is a vicarious act. It is Jesus acting in our place just as he will do in his crucifixion.

What happens in Gethsemane doesn't stay in Gethsemane. Jesus' prayer of grief is given to us as our prayer. We so often struggle to pray. This is why Jesus prays in our place. Whatever we might have experienced in terms of emotional distress or doubt has already been born by Jesus in prayer. He has taken the burden in the fullest and most real sense. And he carries our burdens to the Father in prayer. He prays in verse 39 "yet not what I want but what you want." We do not have the strength to pray this prayer, no matter how hard we try. We cannot muster up a level of obedience this authentic. The most we can manage is "what you want if it is what I want." Yet, because Jesus makes this prayer, his followers can now pray authentically because they don't pray alone: they pray as those who have already had Jesus pray for them. When we pray, Jesus prays. All the things we bring to the Father, including the inauthenticity with which we bring them, including the weakness with which we bring them, are already with the Father in the prayer of Jesus.

Unsurprisingly, theologians take great interest in the events of Gethsemane. How could they not when Jesus' words are so troubling? "My Father, if it is possible, let this cup pass from me" (v. 39). What is clear is the genuineness of Jesus' question. There is no Docetic Christology present here (a heresy that taught Christ only appeared to be human). Jesus wears his heart on his sleeve. He is struggling. He knows that in terms of the big picture, there is little chance of him being able to escape crucifixion now. But as much as he is willing to go through what is before him, he still asks the question.

Jesus' doubts might concern some. They may worry that he seems to have lost sight of the plan. This would be a grave misunderstanding of affairs. His questioning, rather than highlighting imperfection, shows his willingness to go through with the plan. We are more likely to ask questions of someone we trust. This is obedience in relationship—obedience in dialogue. It is a mistake to think Jesus is being passively servile. He will only enter into this if he can do so with his eyes wide open. As an active participant with the Father, he must have communion in prayer with him otherwise this would not be a unified act—a divine act. Going to the cross is to be his work as much as the Father's. And as he continues in prayer, we see something of the will of Father and Son being worked out together. By verse 42 it is resolved, "My Father, if this cannot pass unless I drink it, your will be done."

Jesus is not drinking the cup without knowing of its benefits. He knows its benefit for us—that is why he does it. He enacts the Father's will as his own will; as he says in John 10:30, "I and the Father are one." The divinity of Christ is working in unity with the divinity of the Father. But there is more: Jesus' prayer and action are taking place within a finite brain, made of the same stuff as ours. He is processing as a suffering man who, although not on shut-down mode like the disciples, is struggling to cope. When Jesus prays, it is a human prayer—a prayer offered on our behalf—a prayer given from the bottom of our humanity. Yet he perseveres in prayer. He manages obedience for the sake of those that he and the Father love.

Prayer, even at the best of times, is difficult. Jesus' prayer proves it. He communicates the true nature of prayer—a struggle that expresses the frailty of the human condition. Jesus' persistence in prayer admits struggle but offers what we cannot muster. It is also a prayer of preparation for that which is still to come. He, in an even more shocking sense than in the garden, will go through the worst of what we could ever undergo, but also that which we cannot undergo. Jesus' death is a human death, just as his prayer in the garden is a human prayer. However, it is unique. Only he will undergo this death.

Gethsemane evokes memories of another garden. Long ago, Adam, the first of the human race, shared in the disobedience of his wife Eve. As representatives of humanity, they fell from grace. They brought struggle into the relationship with God. Jesus doesn't go behind Adam and Eve. He doesn't push reset. He enters their struggle. While the first Adam is disobedient in the garden, Jesus is obedient. He is the second Adam. His obedience undoes their disobedience. In fact, his obedience undoes more than just the sin of Adam and Eve. P. T. Forsyth says, "the agony of the garden heals all the agony of the race."[1] What happens in the garden is a global event. Just as the sin of Adam and Eve has disastrous consequences for humanity, so Jesus' remarkable obedience benefits all humanity. Jesus, the cocreator of the world, prays to his Father for the sake of the world; for the sake, therefore, of us; likewise, for the sake of all. He brings our doubt, our emotional distress, and our sin to the Father as his own. He brings our fallen nature to the Father and heals it.

Gethsemane is thus a reality born by Jesus *for us*. When we grasp what is going on here, we see what it does; we begin to take hold of its benefits. Jesus doesn't just *do* something for us; he shows us he *is* for us. He reveals God's heart. That Jesus would obediently and willingly accept our burden himself, bear our emotional distress, our doubts and uncertainties, and make them his own is a remarkable act of divine love. It is an act that shows us we are not ignored, an act that says our concerns are not insignificant or beneath God. These concerns are born by Jesus and more than that, brought before the Father in prayer. They are acted upon and healed through Jesus. The implications of Gethsemane go far and wide. His distress encompasses

1. Forsyth, quoted in Dafydd Jones, *Humanity of Christ*, 244.

the distress of the vulnerable, the poor, and all those in need, just as it encompasses the distress of those who seem to have all they need.

Some might think the garden is a place where we see Jesus so we know how to emulate him—to follow his example. We learn from his obedience, learn what it is like to persevere in prayer. I am sure we can. But I don't want to rush to seeing how we can emulate him. This would take away the *for us* nature of the event. We cannot do what Jesus does here. But we can respond. Because of what Jesus does in the garden, we find new realities opened to us that we can step into. Because Jesus is obedient in the face of great distress, so can we be. We can be obedient because he has been obedient first. Because he has borne our burdens, we can carry the burdens of others. Because he has entered the depths of sorrow, so we can come alongside people in the depths of their sorrow, even the most vulnerable.

Gethsemane should at least show us we can be honest about our emotional distress. Jesus pours himself out for us in humility and vulnerability. He is honest with his Father, which means we can be too, knowing this is not an abomination to him. We see something of what it is to pray here, not just for ourselves but for others. Our prayer is not intercessory for humanity in the same way as Christ's is, but we *can* intercede for others; we can bear the distress of others. Unlike Jesus, we need not do this on our own. We do so as those whose distress has already been born. We do so as those who continue to have this same ascended Christ Jesus as our intercessor in heaven. The garden conveys Christ's intersession for us now. As we focus on it, we see something of his present work.

A remarkable thing about Jesus' prayer is that it doesn't receive an immediate answer from the Father—not audibly at least. He doesn't get an affirmative "It's okay, Son; get through this and you will be resurrected." That answer only comes later. For Jesus, there is no guaranteed way from the garden to the resurrection. There is enough in what he says elsewhere to indicate he hoped he would be resurrected, but this doesn't amount to a guarantee. Jesus does not cheat death through divine foreknowledge. He holds on in hope rather than certainty. It is a mistake to think that because Jesus is divine, Gethsemane is not as serious as it might be. This would be to diminish the significance of his humanity. Nevertheless, because Jesus *has* been raised, even within the midst of human history, he brings hope in a more certain way to us *now*. Because of his cross *and* resurrection, we stand in a different place to where Jesus and the disciples stood in the garden. It is now complete—finished.

What else as a response if he does all this for us? At the end of this passage, one of Jesus' closest followers betrays him. They then bring him before the religious leaders who condemn him to death. Rome condemns him, or is at least indifferent. They place him on a wooden cross, crucifying him on a Godforsaken hill outside the city. But Jesus has prepared himself in prayer. His prayer makes nothing that is coming easy; far from it. However, he has opened himself up before his Father. It is unlikely we will be called to such things, but we can prepare ourselves for whatever is ahead through prayer. We can and must pray, in all our uncertainty, emotional distress, and doubt, as those whose prayers have already been made for us.

When we come to the point of saying, as we inevitably will do, does it have to be like this? Is there no other way? We know Jesus himself has offered this question to the Father already. If we feel alone, there is something for us in the garden. If we feel anxious, there is something for us in the garden. If we are distressed, there is something for us in the garden. If we are doubting, there is something for us in the garden. As we share in the burdens of others, there is something for us here in the garden.

Conclusion

WE SEE THAT THIS Jesus, testified to in Scripture, is remarkable in word, deed, and person. We cannot help but notice this when we look into the garden. Gethsemane makes the most sense if it actually happened. I can imagine that it did. It is likely that Jesus would end up in such a situation, considering where his teaching and actions were heading. That he would go through with it, both here in prayer and later in death, is the more remarkable thing. That it captures our senses is no sufficient reason to question its authenticity. As much as Gethsemane might make sense, these goings-on are strange. They are not the kind of things that could be easily made up.

What we glimpse in the garden is the reality of what Bonhoeffer has called Christ being *for us*—God being for us. We have glimpsed the *homoousion*: the Christ who is for us in the garden is no less than God—of the same being as the Father. Jesus prays and displays emotion as the one who shares our humanity, but also the heart of God. The God who created us human beings intends to dwell fully with humanity. Biblical narratives such as Gethsemane are so much more profound and provocative if Jesus really is the incarnation of the Word, is the reality of God, is the place we must look when we want to know what God is like. This garden also speaks into the seeming hopelessness of the other garden—Eden: the garden that was first good and then lost. What I have said about the Old Testament being prefigural rings true. Eden is transformed; healed; restored, by Christ's obedience in this garden. The garden is deeply good news. It is evangelical theology in intense mode.

Looping back to our question of why still Christian, I can say, why would I not want to be if Christ is so for us—if God's love for the world is such that he becomes so very involved with it? If the garden cannot make sense of the world—of its sufferings and deep mysteries—what can? It speaks at every level into our present experience of the world. Reality looks something like what Jesus and the disciples go through here. Still, the garden challenges us and confronts us. I do not feel comfortable after reading this narrative. This is more than saying that religion is about feeling. What is going on in my emotions relates to the actual events of the narrative as events of revelation. When I glimpse Jesus here, it is as one who has been the recipient of revelation. I am changed. The provocative nature of the Scriptures is all to do with the provocative nature of the central character—Jesus. His life impinges upon our lives and our experiences to the extent whereby our motivations are altered. We must care for those whom he has cared for; we must also share in the burdens, as well as the joys, of others. And as we do, the life of Christ becomes more vivid, more critical, more pressing, to life now.

Part 2

The Spirit

Introduction

I NEED THE HOLY Spirit to be a Christian. This is true by definition and true by conviction. More directly, if the present reality of the Spirit were not part of my experience, I would perhaps cease to be Christian. Thus, we revisit the question we started with, "Why am I *still* a Christian?" So far, my answer has related to Jesus. I have also kept sight of the importance of Scripture. Now I add the experience of the Spirit. When I say the Spirit, I mean the Holy Spirit; the one who is no less than God. We have in the Spirit God's presence with us *now*. But the Spirit is not Jesus. When we speak about Jesus, we have someone physical—visceral—to hold to. We can speak about him in skin and bone; his humanity is not wholly alien to ours. Just so with Scripture. Strange as the world within the pages is, the book itself is in our hands. No such luxury exists with the Holy Spirit.

How do we begin to talk about the Spirit? Even if we refer to the Bible, things are not self-explanatory. At most, we might find a reason to talk about the effects of the Spirit, but "who" the Spirit is, that is another matter. Despite the difficulties, I believe a positive theology of the Holy Spirit is both possible and desirable. In fact, we have every reason to say that in our experience of the Spirit, we can be confident that God is with us. I have already come out as a charismatic Christian. Being charismatic means something in relation to an expectation of the Spirit. The Spirit is always at the forefront. With this in mind, I can convey certain elements of my experience to show what I bring to a theology of the Spirit.

Some charismatics are suspicious of theology. They have their reasons. A previous generation faced skepticism from Christians in all traditions. But times have changed. We are now at a point where most church traditions have seen charismatic renewal sweep into patterns of worship.[1] However, the question of *who* the Spirit is often receives no more attention from charismatics than from anyone else. Some are open to the charismatic in their personal lives, but stop short of assimilating the Spirit into their theology. The challenge facing us is how to integrate experiences of the Spirit into theology. What has been missing from the charismatic tradition is a fully fledged theology of the Holy Spirit. Thankfully, several authors are now addressing this. They will be our dialogue partners as we move forward.

---

1. Sometimes it is more "seep" than "sweep"!

1

Charismatic Spirit

Charismatic Soundings

I HAVE SEEN THE gifts of tongues, healing, and prophecy in operation. I have also practiced such gifts. Some people who came late to the charismatic party say they are surprised when it happens to them. They say it plays havoc with the organized systems they have developed over time. But it has been part of my "normal" for longer than not.

People speak about these charismatic experiences in various ways. Sometimes, they are described as highly emotional and dramatic events, other times, as simple warming of the heart moments. They can be communal or individual. I don't want to offer a detailed analysis of the various phenomena. My interest is in how these experiences leave a mark on our understanding of the Spirit. For those who have such experiences, something is happening that affects how they see God. Just this would seem to merit attention.

There are legitimate criticisms posed to this form of worship from various quarters, Christian and otherwise. I share some of these concerns. However, waiting on and receiving the Spirit is something I acknowledge *positively* as part of my theological framework. I still desire these experiences. I hope they will keep informing me.

We should acknowledge that there was a theology of the Holy Spirit long before the charismatic and Pentecostal movements. It can become a problem when we charismatics imply an insider knowledge of the Spirit. It implies others have missed out or misunderstood. It is almost as though we are saying the Spirit is not manifest in other forms of church. Such thinking can be harmful. There have always been Christians who have sought after the Spirit in profound ways. For example, quiet, contemplative prayer has long focused on the Spirit. Such practices may not have the immediacy or drama of the charismatic, but they are no less significant. Likewise, if we are intent on seeing immanent experience as the deciding factor of authenticity we can neglect the role of the Spirit in key areas such as the doctrine of adoption. This is a concern. It makes the Spirit only about phenomena. Thus, as we proceed, I want to integrate classical ways of considering the Spirit with charismatic understandings.

Charismatic and Systematic

My story includes profound encounters with the Spirit that have left a mark on my understanding of *who* the Spirit is and thus who God is. When I think about God now, it is through a filter that includes charismatic experience of the Holy Spirit. Talking like this inevitably gets us into the realm of systematic theology. This is the branch of theology with the laudable, if always unrealistic aim of making sense of the whole. Some mistake it for trying to make things too ordered. However, what systematic theologians are doing is saying that there should be some kind of coherency to our talk about God. It is an important endeavor and I think it *can* be related to what we experience.

When I talk about God, I cannot separate this talk from feelings. These feelings are heightened in charismatic worship: I get emotional; I experience desire—yearning even. Where do these emotions come from and how do they relate to the Spirit? Emotions such as longing and desire are fraught with problems. Some of the problems have already been identified in relation to experience. Desire is too subjective, too emotive, not grounded enough in God's word. To add to the problem, desire has sexual connotations. This puts some people right off. But as said, we cannot avoid starting from experience, and our experience in charismatic worship often involves intimacy and desire.

Sarah Coakley gives due space to this sense of desire in her theology. Her *God, Sexuality and the Self* is worthy of particular attention. She insists that language of vulnerability, waiting, risk and intimacy, expresses something of the way of the Spirit. We shouldn't detach our emotions from our recognition of who the Spirit is. Coakley is successful in capturing the essence of charismatic experience. Being in the Spirit is an assault on the senses. It feels like something. It seems bordering on scandalous to say our feelings for God should be spoken of in such a way—as reliable interpreters of God's character. Nevertheless, by doing so, we give the depth of charismatic encounter experienced its due recognition and therefore give the work of the Spirit due recognition. The contribution of the charismatic renewal is that it puts such emotions back on the agenda. Language of closeness is not anti-theological; it is rather a fitting explanation of our relation to the Spirit. Intimacy of experience implies a God whose Spirit is active amongst the community of believers—a God who is very much alive and present.

Coakley also describes the Spirit's work as an "interruption."[1] The Spirit interrupts our ordered formalities. In the moment of encounter, our priorities are shifted—our vision of God and each other changes. Sometimes our collective worship is taken off script for the sake of a deeper encounter with God. We hunger for such occasions in charismatic expressions. It is not *just* an experience that people are seeking in these moments. They are recognizing the transformative work of the Holy Spirit. It isn't just an in-the-moment thing. People's lives can be taken off script post-encounter. I hope for these sorts of moments and celebrate them. Indeed, the charismatic movement itself is an important interruption of church life.

I am not advocating that we should base everything on emotions. If our focus were solely on how we feel, we wouldn't be talking about God anymore; we would be talking about ourselves. But the Spirit gives a safeguard. Yes, the Spirit ignites our desire and draws us to intimacy with God. But, as Coakley points out, the Spirit also purifies our emotions and thoughts. This is biblical. The fruit of the Spirit includes self-discipline (1 Tim 1:7). Receiving the Spirit is not only about feeling something, it is about being transformed and renewed. The Spirit stops desire becoming inappropriate—stops us merely projecting our wishes onto God as though God is an extension of our emotions. We can say that God desires intimacy, but this is not an out-of-control affair. The Spirit of God is also in the business of making our desires *right* desires.

Another danger in emphasizing intimacy is that we can cease to recognize God's freedom and otherness. Coakley holds intimacy together with an apophatic approach to theology. Apophatic theology recognizes the importance of divine mystery. It gives attention to who God is *not* as much as who God *is*. She says this is appropriate in relation to experiences of the Spirit. In such encounters, we find a sense of "unknowing" as much as a

---

1. Coakley, *God, Sexuality*, 87–88.

sense of knowing.[2] We don't come away from such experiences as masters of understanding but as those struck by mystery. If we recognize the mysterious nature of God and are cautious with desire, then we only give desire its due—we don't impede God's freedom.

Mystery is important, but I think Coakley overemphasizes it. Insisting on mystery doesn't get us out of the danger of becoming subject to our own desires. If God is unknown, then we are even more at the mercy of our thoughts and feelings. If we turn to the thought of Paul in the New Testament, we see that his interest is in a God who *has* made himself known. In response to the altar to the unknown God in view (Acts 17), he announces a God who is very much known, specifically through the resurrected Christ.[3] With Christ, we talk about a God who is known, not just in mystery, but in reality. Christ has inhabited our knowable space. This is the reality of the incarnation. As I will say later, we cannot separate our talk of the Spirit from our talk of Christ. The Spirit is one with the incarnate, resurrected, and ascended Jesus. As Christ comes to be known, so does the Spirit. We can be confident, therefore, that our experiences of the Spirit are telling us something about who the Spirit is.

Pentecost tells us that God wants to be known. As much as there is great mystery in the phenomenal happenings of that day, there is no holding back on God's part. Despite the perplexity of many, the tongues heard are native—they are to be understood. And Peter explains it. He doesn't say "today you've encountered a mystery." No, he concludes thus: "let the entire house of Israel *know with certainty* that God has made him both Lord and Messiah."[4] The Spirit present at Pentecost is for the understanding of the whole earth; at least, that is, for those who can receive it. The human race in all its diverse manifestations gets the Holy Spirit. Peter wants to explain it not only because he is struck by the mystery—he is struck by what God is saying—by who the Spirit is. This same event of knowing happens in charismatic encounter. It is not coincidental that it feels like we are getting to know God in these moments. I don't just come away with a sense of wonder at the mystery, but with the feeling that a relationship is being built.

It is an outrageous claim in one sense, but Scripture teaches us that as the Spirit is poured out, we encounter God not just in mystery but also in person. The Spirit I encounter draws me to God the Son, gives

---

2. Coakley, *God, Sexuality*, 43–45.

3. Joshua McNall makes this point in "Shrinking Pigeon, Brooding Dove," 295–308.

4. Acts 2:36 (italics mine).

understanding, facilitates communion. That this is the case might be a mystery, but the God we encounter is not *only* mystery. Again, this relates to why I want to be Christian. Not because I am drawn to mystery, but because the love of Christ in the Spirit lets me in; because in the moment of encounter there is a feeling both that I am known and that I am coming to know.

There is a place for the language of mystery. Acknowledging mystery means we don't claim to possess God on our own terms. Coakley is rightly responding to our need to be in control. When we are in the Spirit, we recognize that we are not in control. This is good. God is not to be hemmed in or made to do things at our bidding. Part of the power of charismatic worship is the letting go of our emotions for the sake of connecting with the Spirit. In the freedom we experience, we come to recognize that God is free. Nevertheless, what we experience in terms of God's love and friendship in this letting go speaks of a communicating God, a personal God, a revealing God. Coakley's recognition of the importance of risky, uncontrolled devotion of the desires to God is important. But we need not fear for God's freedom when we say that in these emotional moments, we are seeing a clearer picture of God. God's involvement is an act of love—an act of communication. Who are we, therefore, to say God must remain unknown?[5]

Coakley allows experience of the Spirit to resource her theology. In fact, she suggests that the Spirit could be our starting point as we approach the doctrine of the Trinity. If the experience of the Spirit is fundamental to what Christian faith is—who God is—then why not start with the Spirit? We have too long treated the Spirit, she says, as the "problematic 'third'" in the Trinity.[6] We somehow think we are on safer territory speaking of the Father and the Son. We are nervous when speaking of the Spirit. We find what we say of the Spirit is difficult to relate to Father and Son. Thus, through our ordering of language, we have implied that the Spirit is the least of the Triune persons. Coakley's point is provocative, but I think she is right. Certainly, we could allow the Spirit—or at least prayer in the Spirit—to be a starting point for theology. Our encounter with God does invariably start here. This goes alongside what I have said about Christ before now. We don't diminish the importance of Christ by saying it is the Spirit who enables our encounter with God. Indeed, Christ's reality becomes more vivid in the light of Spirit encounter. Just as the Spirit and

---

5. I will explore this more in part 3.

6. Coakley, *God, Sexuality*, 334.

Christ share in the same essence, so our encounter with the Spirit facilitates our recognition of Christ.

Allowing the Spirit to be a starting point means we permit what we experience—what we desire—to come to the fore. But how much should we give over to desire? A charismatic adage says, "Let go and let God." As important as desire is and as much as I find the emotional elements of charismatic experience formative, I recognize that desire is faulty. When we "let go," therefore, what or who are we letting go to? We might just be giving in to ourselves if we let go, and that gets us nowhere. To what extent does our letting go trigger the activity of the Spirit? Coakley suggests that participation with God in the Spirit requires a "posture of contemplative 'effacement.'"[7] By this, she means a reduction of the self in order to give space to the Spirit. I at least agree that the less we make of ourselves, the less we try to control God. However, this posture of worship, this making less of ourselves, this giving room for God, is not something *we* enact. We cannot make more of God. God is not dependent on us. Receiving the Spirit is not about *our* making room, but about the Spirit acting in grace towards us. For charismatic worship, this means that when we encounter the Spirit, we do so on the Spirit's own terms. We do not become elevated in the Spirit through self-negation. Rather, our making less of ourselves is a *response* to the work of the Spirit. The Apostle John reminds us that the "wind blows wherever it pleases" (John 3:8). By this, he means the Spirit. If it is about our self-reduction and not the Spirit's free action, then we have lost sight of the Spirit. We have also made too much of ourselves.

Nevertheless, as the Spirit comes, my desires are inclined towards intimacy. It might be that this says something about me, but what does it say about God? As soon as we ask this, we are into theology. We are saying that God the Holy Spirit desires intimacy. God is intimate. This is a claim too far for some. It comes too close to implying a vulnerability or openness on God's part. It becomes even more of a problem when we talk about experiences of uncontrollability in the Spirit. By admitting uncontrollability, we are suggesting something profound about who the Spirit of God is and who we are in relationship with the Spirit. God acts in a way that cannot be systematized.

The charismatic experience testifies to a profound depth of relationship with the Spirit. It testifies to the fluid dynamism of God's ongoing interaction with those created in his image. Here is a lively God who desires

---

7. Coakley, *God, Sexuality*, 23.

to be known and reflected in vibrant worship. Here is a God who does not exert control, a God who can well cope with unpredictability in us humans, who is happy for us to not feel in control; a God who can communicate in vulnerability whilst still being God. There will be more to say about knowing God, but we can at least say here that the experience of the Spirit testifies to a revealing God—a personal God. In saying this much, we only confirm what is there in Scripture.

Trouble in the Waters

We cannot ignore the problems of defining the Spirit by our experience, but they are not insurmountable. It is important to identify the problems as it has a direct bearing on who we conceive the Spirit to be. I have highlighted the danger of measuring true spirituality by how much we use the charismatic gifts. If the gifts are the sole identifier of having received the Spirit then what about those who haven't received? Are they without the Spirit? No—I don't think so. The biblical pattern of the Spirit—the narrative of Pentecost—is contrary to exclusion. If we define the terms of how the Spirit is received, or what outcomes there have been, then we no longer recognize the freedom of the Spirit, nor do we acknowledge the Spirit's nature as gift.

I have had intense and lasting experiences of the Spirit in contexts where there was no recognition of the charismatic. The most vivid experience was during a Sunday Eucharist at Lancaster Priory. The communion host came into the midst of the congregation—God's presence amid the people. There were smells and there were bells. Incense filled the space, just as the Spirit fills all things. The silence, punctuated by the ringing of bells, recognition of the presence of Christ and the Spirit. The intensity of encounter was phenomenal, not least for me. The formality of the service was no barrier to a sense of awe and wonder at the majesty and love of God. This high church formality contrasted with my low church background. But it was beautiful and real. God was there. After the service, I spoke to people about their faith. Some were just looking in, having caught something of the beauty. They were happy to be there, even though they were not sure they yet had a faith of their own. Others were theologically persuaded of this approach to the Eucharist. For them, this was the church as it should be. Regardless of people's perception, the Spirit's presence was intense and tangible. We cannot confine the work of the Spirit to charismatic manifestations.[8] To do so would be to discount occasions, common among the life of believers, such as these.

The Spirit's work is powerfully present in the diverse expressions of the church and not limited to a particular type of worship. Likewise, the Spirit's work is worldwide. In these last days, says the prophet Joel, "I will pour out my Spirit on all flesh" (Joel 2:28). This could mean several things, but at the very least, the reality of the pouring out of the Spirit comes first, the manifestations second (sons and daughters prophesying, etc.). The Spirit is poured out on all flesh, active in drawing all people to God. Yes, this can result in ecstatic manifestation, but if we confine the Spirit to charismatic experiences, we no longer recognize the global outpouring testified to in Acts that draws all people together.

Just as the Spirit is not all about manifestations, so the Spirit is not all about victory and overcoming. When we get carried away in the euphoria of charismatic excess, we sometimes leave little room for doubt and vulnerability. Power can be prioritized over gentleness, reflectiveness or suffering. I have seen this—not least in some of our song lyrics. The Spirit becomes the key to success in life, helping the believer overcome every problem that comes their way. Leaders in this context can succumb to the impression that they must enable this victory—this overcoming. They unintentionally feel the need to become the facilitator for the Spirit's work, the one who enables things to happen—to move the meeting towards an empowering Spirit encounter. The problem comes when there are no tangible phenomena. The implication is that there is a problem or a blockage. Somebody has done something wrong, whether leader or recipient. This is particularly difficult for those who never have dramatic experiences. It leaves them in the cold.

Some of us are easily whipped up into a frenzy over the Spirit's presence. I have often been carried away. In the moment, it is like this presence can overcome anything. But for those left behind, those who do not experience heightened joy, the signs point towards failure. These same people are often the most vulnerable—the ones who can be most damaged. The vulnerable being left behind contradicts everything that Christ is about. If Christ and the Spirit are in cooperation, which they surely are, then the Spirit is not so much with the winners in life, but with the broken. Coakley has concerns about charismatic expressions that overemphasize notions of

8. Andrew Wilson talks of a similar experience from a charismatic perspective. See Wilson, *Spirit and Sacrament*, 56.

victory: "Is the Spirit only to be a 'triumphalist' Spirit, bearer of joy and positive 'feeling'? Or, if this is Christ's Spirit, breathed out of his scarred body, 'one in being' (*homoousion*) with Father and Son, must one not allow as much for the fir of purgation . . . as for the refreshment of the comforting dove?"[9] The Spirit may well enable feelings of euphoria and positivity, and often does, but this is not all. The Spirit also draws us to the life of Christ in the world, including his suffering. The Spirit may, for example, draw us to conviction and repentance. Likewise, the Spirit will draw us to others, just as Christ exists for others. If we are in the Spirit, we will surely reflect who the Spirit is about and be inclined towards them.

A central hallmark of the charismatic church is its emphasis on physical and psychological healing. When the church gathers, there is an expectation that such healing will take place. Public prayer reflects this expectation—we expect something to happen. This is not unique to charismatic or Pentecostal circles, but its imminent likelihood is emphasized through our language. The great strength of this expectation is that it recovers a part of early Christian practice seen both in the ministry of Jesus and in the accounts of the early church in Acts. I agree with this recovery of emphasis. However, the implication can be that healing in the Spirit is some kind of given. It is as though if true faith is present, all illness disappears. This is troubling. It is grim for those who don't get healed. Further, it implies that suffering is alien to God's will. To say this, would be to contradict the cross, contradict God's identification with suffering, contradict the reality of life, contradict Christ's cry in Gethsemane. If an overemphasis on the certainty of healing contradicts the cross, it is contrary to the work of the Spirit. The Spirit is not at odds with the Son. This is not to dismiss the possibility, or even likelihood, of healing. But this possibility needs to be understood in relation to God's loving gift, not as something that is ours to give if we only have enough faith. We pray *hoping* the Spirit will heal, but we do not presume of the Spirit. In this way we honor God and honor those we pray for.

A final concern is a tendency to prioritize the extraordinary over the ordinary. It is as though if nothing extraordinary has happened, something has gone wrong. In my first encounters with the charismatic, there were times where it was as if the whole worship service was designed to create a high point of Holy Spirit intimacy. If no such height came, people felt let down. Desiring intimacy is good, but judging the authenticity of worship

9. Coakley, *God, Sexuality*, 180.

by the level of intimacy reached is a problem. It means the Spirit becomes no more than a fulfiller of wants and needs. Surely, the Spirit is no mere psychological fix to fill the void in our lives. Even more seriously, we are in danger of making the Spirit an idol—one who no longer comes in freedom, being instead subject to our whims.

Despite the pitfalls, I think there is great value in desiring charismatic experiences of the Spirit. The chief contribution of charismatic worship is what it engenders in terms of vulnerability, unpredictability, disarming intimacy and dynamism. All this should lead us to Christ and subsequently to others. If it is only ever about ourselves, then we have got the wrong person—the wrong Spirit. Affirming the liberating work of the Spirit is different to emphasizing positivistic and triumphalist aspects of Spirit encounter. It is also different to limiting Spirit experience to a heartwarming sense of peace. The possibility of healing and of the so-called charismatic gifts is something I want to affirm. However, everything is a gift—both the phenomena involved and the resulting impact on us as the worshiping community. Not a gift because we are charismatic, but because there is something about the Spirit that results in these gifts being manifest. The Spirit is an unconditional giver. Desiring the gifts is good; desiring intimacy is good. We have every reason to expect that the Spirit, in being poured out on all flesh, desires this too. When Jesus says he is leaving with us an advocate, the promised Holy Spirit, we assume he is leaving us with someone like himself.[10] We assume that this someone—the Holy Spirit—is God, just as Christ is. This is the Spirit who we desire, who we encounter and who we intimately relate to in our worship.

Being Christian is not appealing if I am only drawn to myself. Likewise, being Christian is not about being on the winning side: the side with the best psychological fix; the side where the true worshipers find their problems disappearing. Being in the presence of the Spirit is so refreshing because we are pulled out of ourselves and towards others. The manifest presence of the Spirit makes God's heart for all people fresh to us in the moment. We see an altogether more compelling vision of what it means to be human. It is another reason to be Christian. Being in the Spirit means being drawn into the things of God, it is knowing God and therefore knowing who God is for. God desires us as fellow partners and puts in us the desire for others to come too.

---

10. See John 14:26.

2

Spirit in Person

Christ and Spirit

WHEN I THINK ABOUT the Spirit, someone like Jesus comes into view. When I experience the Spirit, I experience something entirely like the love of Christ. Christ and Spirit are wrapped up together. This is a theological point. When Christ and the Father give the Spirit, they are giving of themselves. The Spirit is distinct in personhood, yes, but in "being," no. The Spirit is never at odds with Jesus Christ. This means that our theology of the Spirit needs grounding in Christ—specifically, in his incarnation. What we say of Christ defines what we say of the Spirit. Not only this, but the Spirit is operative in Christ's incarnation; the same Spirit, in fact, that we experience in the charismatic. To get the Holy Spirit, it is therefore necessary to see how the same Spirit is active within Jesus' specific earthly ministry. As we see this, we can also see how through the work of the Spirit, the reality of Christ is present to us today. In Christ and Spirit, we know that God is for us now.

In *This Incredibly Benevolent Force*, Cornelius van der Kooi discusses the Spirit from the perspective of Reformed Theology; in particular, the Spirit in relation to Christ. He explores two types of Christology: Logos Christology and Spirit Christology. Logos Christology is to do with the eternal Word made flesh. It has been the primary way of talking about Christ for theologians through the ages. It takes Christ's divinity as its foundation. Spirit Christology, although compatible, has a different starting point. Christ's life is seen through the work of the Spirit in him.[1] Spirit Christology is valuable for several reasons. It helps us understand both the Spirit and Christ more fully. We can see that the Spirit enables Christ's

1. Van der Kooi, *This Incredibly Benevolent Force*, 22–23 and 34–38.

51

perfect relationship with the Father. Yes, the Son is in unity with the Father, but the Spirit's active involvement is essential. This applies, for example, to Christ's earthly seeking after the Father. The Spirit draws the life of Christ to the Father and in turn empowers Christ's life in the flesh. As the Spirit-indwelt human, Christ's role mirrors the Spirit's activity in the world. His ministry looks like the ministry of the Spirit.

We see the heart of the Spirit, for example, when Christ heals or casts out evil. The heart of the Spirit is to bring liberty to all those in bondage. Jesus enacts the Spirit's liberative desire. This means that with a Spirit Christology, Jesus' miracles are not so much about his innate divinity, but cooperative acts with the Spirit—acts that say something about who the Spirit is. The miracles are thus not primarily to do with Christ being the divine Word; they are more to do with what the Spirit is doing for the world in, with, and through Christ.

A Spirit Christology need not undermine Christ's divinity, but relate it to the ongoing activity of the Spirit in the world. A Spirit Christology is more reflective of historical context. The Spirit empowers Christ for life in the world in that moment. In a Spirit Christology, Christ's fleshly existence is taken seriously as empowered by the Spirit. Christ is still the preexistent one, but his uniqueness is not only explained through his being the eternal Word. Christ's unique words and deeds relate not only to his divinity but also to his anointing in the Spirit.

I often hear it said that the miracles of Jesus are proof of his divinity. The problem with this is what it does to Christ's humanity. It is as though he is cheating. It puts his identification with us at stake. But when we say it is the Spirit at work bringing healing or casting out demons, we see that his reality is not so far from ours. He is doing these things as the fully human one. We too can understand the Spirit as the one who brings release and healing because we have seen the Spirit at work. For charismatic and Pentecostal expressions of church, miracles are expected phenomena. When we see them, we gain a sight of the life of Christ in the world. We also see that he would have us act in cooperation with the Spirit. This does not mean that Christ is like us only closer to the Spirit. Nevertheless, in becoming like us, he acts out his ministry in dependence on the activity of the Spirit.

We need not look at Christ's physical deeds and conclude they must be down to his divinity. Nevertheless, we do see his divinity in them when we consider *why* he is doing these things. Christ and the Spirit's activity in the world expresses Gods' being *for* the world. Jesus *wants* to heal people because that is what divine love looks like. He *can* heal people because of the Spirit. Divinity is in the meaning of his deeds, not in their impressiveness. From this perspective, we see that both Christ and Spirit exist for us. If the miracles of Jesus only proved he was divine, they would be self-serving, about the glory of God more than the liberation and healing of us humans.

To take this point to its conclusion, it is worth considering how tales of the miraculous are narrated in the charismatic church. Although it is not my intention to shift practice here, certain questions are worth considering. If we pray for miracles to happen, what are we praying for? If we see the miraculous, what are we seeing? Are we seeing the power of God at work? Are we witnessing proof of God's existence? Maybe. But more importantly, we are seeing *who* God is for. We are catching something of what it is to want people to be made whole; be made well; be made new. It then becomes less about the impressiveness of miracles and more about what the Spirit is *for*, in enabling them.

What else is the Spirit doing through Christ? Just as Christ disrupts our agendas and reconfigures our imaginations, so does the Spirit. The Spirit is a "protagonist in the life of the church."[2] Christ is for us, but in being for us, challenges us and redirects us. Just so with the Spirit. The Spirit is disruptive. The Spirit has the power to redirect our priorities. We understand Christ and Spirit mutually in this way. Through what we encounter in charismatic worship, we come to know both Christ and Spirit. Our experience of the Spirit helps us understand the Jesus of the Gospels. Without having experienced the Spirit personally, it might be more difficult to see these things—to see the charismatic elements of Christ's ministry. Understood like this, charismatic experience need not be separate from serious biblical scholarship. The two can go hand in hand. The events witnessed to in Scripture become events we can sense because we have witnessed these things too.

Emphasizing Spirit Christology allows us to see how the Word assumed weak and vulnerable flesh. As the Spirit is the uniting love of God acting eternally within the Godhead, so the Spirit facilitates God's movement towards us through Christ's incarnation. Christ, anointed by the Spirit, shares our frail nature. The Spirit enables Christ's unity with the Father and thus facilitates Christ to fulfill God's unity with us. The Spirit is the perfecting agent of Christ's life in the flesh, empowering him to offer in our place the work of salvation and atonement. We have seen that the incarnation says something profound about God—that God risks his nature for the

2. Van der Kooi, *This Incredibly Benevolent Force*, 38.

53

sake of our nature. Just so with the pouring out of the Spirit. The Spirit is the means of God's movement towards us. This is the same Spirit hovering over the waters at creation, the same presence of God who dwelt with Israel. This same Spirit is now amongst the church, enabling us to fulfill God's purposes in the world.

Just as the Spirit is at work in Christ, so the Spirit is at work in us. As the Spirit empowers Christ's remarkable acts, so the Spirit does such things through us. We are not the same as Christ, but the Spirit binds us to him and we thus become participants. Van der Kooi sees these acts of the Spirit in us as events of sanctification. The Reformed Church is used to saying that the Spirit is the one who sanctifies. In the same way, the Spirit is the transformative agent in the miraculous—in the supernatural.[3] The sanctifying work of the Spirit among us is grace. The charismatic, rather than being at odds with this, is complementary. It recognizes the diverse manifestations of this transformative and sanctifying Spirit. Healing, charismatic gifts, etc., are for our sanctification. They display who we are becoming as the Spirit-filled community.

Because Christ is anointed with the Spirit, we can be too. Christ gives the Spirit—brings the Spirit within reach. Christ accomplishes our salvation, but the Spirit puts this in us. The Spirit, Romans 8 tells us, is the Spirit of adoption. We are adopted through the Spirit. This doesn't mean we have the same relationship enjoyed by Father, Son, and Spirit, but it comes close. Through our adoptive relation, we can know something of the Triune love of God. And we are more than passive recipients. Our adoption enables participation. We are able to actively lean into the gift of the Spirit. Our participation also requires something of us. We find that we must be open to the way of the Spirit. It is even incumbent on us to pursue the Spirit. Charismatic worship prioritizes this leaning in, giving due attention to our adoption as children of the Spirit. When we look for signs of the Spirit, therefore, we act as the adopted children we are.

Our experience of the Spirit relates to our experience of Christ. In fact, if we do not give due attention to Christ, then we are not giving due attention to the Holy Spirit. Put differently, our experiences of the Spirit are false if they do not relate to Christ. This means our leaning into the Spirit should not become indulgent. It cannot be experience for experience's sake. If it becomes this, then it loses the sharpness and challenge of Christ's life. Just as we can see Christ in the light of the Spirit, so we can see the Spirit in

---

3. Van der Kooi, *This Incredibly Benevolent Force*, 112–13.

the light of Christ. Christ lives as one anointed by the Spirit. Likewise, the Spirit's life and activity come into view when we look at Christ.

I have known times of being kept alert to the world by the Spirit. An occurrence of my early adult year's is worth reflecting on to illustrate the point. As a teenager, I didn't think I wanted to go to university. It seemed too disconnected from the real world. Having no real motivation, I didn't even make it through sixth form college. Without a view of what to do next, I spent a year volunteering for my church. Towards the end of the year, I went on a week of mission just outside Manchester. It started with an evening of worship and prayer. During the meeting, the love and peace of God overwhelmed me to the point of debilitation. Feeling elated, I lay down and soaked it in.

It would be easy to explain this experience without God. Away from home, I had invested my energy and emotions in the week; I felt accepted by the group of people around me; I was looking for somewhere to place my value. Such things are likely to affect one's emotional state. Despite these possible explanations, I attribute this experience to the work of the Holy Spirit. It had the hallmarks of a charismatic experience.

If this were an isolated experience, it wouldn't say very much. But a strikingly different experience followed. The next day, I went with a group of other keen young Christian adults to a deprived housing estate on the edge of Manchester. We had a mobile youth center in the shape of a doubledecker bus that we parked right in the center of the estate next to a park. The children and teenagers of the estate swarmed the bus, and we spent a good number of hours chatting with them, playing games, sports, etc. Nothing like this, they told us, had been put on for them before. They were perceptibly moved. The time came to leave, but they didn't want us to go. A small crowd of young people climbed onto the little car in which some of us were attempting to leave. I broke into tears, feeling the sadness and hopelessness of these young people. It went right through me. I felt the Holy Spirit, the Spirit of Christ, well up within me stirring compassion for these teenagers: teenagers who, as far as I can see from reading the Gospels, would have flocked to Jesus. Bizarrely, they were flocking to us.

I have relayed this story to my students over the years. They find it moving, but few attach the Spiritual significance to it that I do. I see it as an experience of the Holy Spirit—another charismatic experience. Together, these experiences changed my life. A few months later, I moved into a similar estate in Manchester and lived and worked there for three years, ministering to teenagers and families. Ever since, I have related the experience of the Spirit to the reality of Christ's existence in the world. The Spirit does nothing that wouldn't make sense outside of the reality of Christ. The seemingly indulgent enjoyment of the night before was drawn towards the reality of Christ the day after.

That the Spirit is a person who shares life with the Son and Father means we cannot look for experiences of the Spirit in isolation. Christianity is not just something that puts us in touch with the spiritual. Likewise, Charismatic Christianity is not just a new form of spirituality. We must look at the person of the Spirit as coequal with Father and Son. The reason I attach particular significance to the experiences mentioned is that they make coherent sense within a Christ-centered framework. They make sense in relation to the Christ of the Gospels. I treat them as more than emotional experiences explainable by circumstances. If Christ was walking the earth today, in the power of the Spirit, he might be moved by these young people in Manchester. The Spirit might want someone to live and work amongst such people. In fact, Christ *is* acting in the world through the Spirit leading us towards such as these.

Charismatic experience can be significant in the life of the believer. Its authenticity lies in its relation to the reality of Christ in the world. But if it is *only* a moving emotional experience, then it is not yet the Holy Spirit, because it does not have the challenge of Christ's reality present within it. We can pause again here and consider the question "Why still Christian?" In an experience of the Spirit, something is happening that both confirms and challenges. The Spirit awakens my desires and hopes. Everything points to the fact that my encounter is real. I am drawn into the love of God, the one who is at work in the world now. As I experience this love and its transformative power, Jesus Christ makes more and more sense. The Spirit also unsettles and redirects me, pulls me out of myself, joins me to the life of Christ, directs me towards others. I want to be Christian because of the way it helps me look at the world. Indifference to the world becomes impossible. I don't want to ignore the people in whom the Spirit takes an interest; I want to catch a heart for the same people who Christ moved towards.

Where is the Spirit?

In a Spirit Christology, the Spirit's location is the incarnate Son. Even today, the place of the Spirit is the resurrected and ascended Christ. But there is more to say about the "where" of the Spirit. Where else is the Spirit? Old and New Testaments are scattered with examples of the Spirit's presence in the world, from the waters of creation, to the voice that has something to say to the churches spread through the world.[4] Thus, what we say of the Spirit, although grounded in Christ, cannot be limited to the physical location of Jesus. The risen Son sends the Spirit in his place. The Spirit now dwells with us here on earth. The Spirit fills the earth. We could say the Spirit is omnipresent—in all places at all times. But the Spirit is more than a non-material presence that happens to be everywhere. If we only focus on the omnipresence of the Spirit, we do little justice to the vibrant life of this person who is actively involved in the community of believers. If we say the Spirit is in every place, we must do so in a way that does justice to the Spirit's personhood.

In former times, the temple in Jerusalem was where God's Spirit—God's presence—dwelt on earth. It was the epicenter of faith and life. N. T. Wright notes that prayer and worship, for example, were directed to the temple. It was where heaven and earth met and hence the focal point for God's community.[5] The Jewish community, although spread throughout the earth, returned at various points in the year to the temple. But because there was dissatisfaction with the temple, it was normal in the first century to ask, "Where is God's presence now?" It is no wonder, therefore, that Zechariah is so surprised when an angel shows up in God's dwelling place, right by the altar of incense. We are told that he "was terrified, and fear overwhelmed him."[6] The expectation that God was present in the temple had obviously dropped. God wasn't where he was supposed to be. For Wright, this cannot be abstracted from the fact that people were being excluded from the temple system; the very people God was most interested in. These same people were hoping, longing, for something to change, for God to return. Little did Zechariah know that such a return was imminent.

In Jesus, the return of God to his people was taking place. Christ's earthly ministry, empowered by the Spirit, was God being amid the people again. Jesus was the new dwelling place of the living God.[7] Jesus didn't leave his people without God's presence when he departed: as he went to the Father, he gave the promised Holy Spirit. The return of God's presence

4. Gen 1:2; Rev 2–3.
5. Wright, *Paul and the Faithfulness*, 365.
6. Luke 1:12.
7. Wright, *Jesus and the Victory*, 631–44.

to the people in Christ continues at Pentecost. Not only that, a whole new community is built.

When Paul meets Christ on route to Damascus, he knows God's presence is back. He doesn't bother too much about having missed out on Christ's pre-crucifixion ministry. He doesn't get jealous of those who walked with him on the shore of Galilee. He hears the voice of the risen Jesus.[8] He knows he is in the presence of God. Christ's ascension to the Father doesn't speak of God's absence. God's presence is just as personal, just as dynamic, and just as real, in the person of the Spirit.

For Paul, the newly birthed church becomes the temple of the living God—the dwelling place of God's Spirit. Paul knows that the Spirit, who was at work in Christ, is now at work amongst God's new community. That is why he can ask: "Do you not know that you are God's temple and that God's Spirit dwells in you?" (1 Cor 3:6). There is a dynamic transfer of the Spirit's location: from temple, to Christ, to Christ's followers. The Spirit might be everywhere, but the epicenter shifts. Worship and prayer are no longer directed to the temple. Christians celebrate and acknowledge that where people are praying and worshiping, there too is the Spirit. Wright says that prayer "'in the spirit' was the equivalent of turning towards the Temple."[9] What was going on in prayer in the early church was what had been going on in the temple—God's people were meeting with him. But the difference is radical. Prayer in the Spirit now happens wherever two or three are gathered in Christ's name just as he said it would.[10]

The church is the dwelling place of the Spirit on earth. This was a provocative claim in Paul's day. It still is. It has major implications for what takes place in prayer. Prayer in the Spirit is prayer familiar to charismatics. This can be seen at its most vivid in Romans 8:1–30. Wright summarizes Paul thus: Prayer "in the Spirit would lead to that strange and powerful sense of "groaning" in which the groaning of the whole creation, and of God's people with that, seemed to be taken up into the groaning of God."[11] Groaning displays a longing for God's presence among the people. This is the pattern of New Testament prayer. The early church yearned for the Spirit so deeply because the Spirit promises to be amongst them.

---

8. Acts 9:1–6.

9. Wright, *Paul and the Faithfulness*, 365.

10. Matt 18:20.

11. Wright, *Paul and the Faithfulness*, 365.

Where is the Spirit? The Spirit is in Christ. The Spirit is also where we gather in Christ's name. Longing and desire play an important part in this encounter. They are a response to the Spirit's being with us. The Spirit is there to be yearned for, groaned for, longed for. We can expect the Spirit's presence based on God's track record of dealing with his people. We can also say that the Spirit's presence amongst us is not only mystery—it is what we should have always expected. That doesn't mean the Spirit is predictable or mundane. The Spirit is living and dynamic. We don't bring in God's presence, but what we have said about the Spirit points towards God's presence with his people when they gather. Charismatic worship does not usher in the Spirit. It is more a response to the promise of the Spirit. I enjoy being with this same Spirit. I can testify to the Spirit's closeness. If the Spirit is among us, then we shouldn't be surprised if our experiences—in worship, in prayer—are personal, meaningful, and emotional. And just as the Spirit is poured out on the whole earth, so will the community of God's people go to the earth as they receive the Spirit.

Who is the Spirit?

We charismatics often talk about the *presence* of the Spirit but this is different than talking about the *person* of the Spirit. Put differently, we talk more about "what" the Spirit does than "who" the Spirit is. We said the same of Christ—that the "who" question is key—but it is even more necessary with the Spirit. We can begin by saying who the Spirit is not. The Spirit is not worldly in the same way as Christ. Therefore, when we speak of the Spirit, we are not *only* saying what is true of the Son. As much as I have tried to insist on interpreting the work of the Spirit through the work of Christ, we cannot completely conflate the Spirit and Christ. As Colin Gunton says, the Spirit might be "active *within* the world" in the same way as Christ, but this does not mean that the Spirit is "identical with any part of the world."[12] The Spirit is not time bound, not physical. The Spirit blows where the Spirit will.

The unique nature of the Spirit poses a challenge, because if I can only talk about my *experiences* I am not yet talking about who the Spirit is. I am just talking about myself—about my worldly existence. If the Spirit and the world are distinct, then where does knowledge of the Spirit come from? One place we might start is with Augustine's various considerations of the Spirit in his classic work *On the Trinity.* Adam Kotsko highlights three

12. Gunton, *Theology Through the Theologians*, 108.

particular characteristics given attention by Augustine: "love," "gift," and "enjoyment."[13] By considering what Augustine says, we can focus on this question of "who" the Spirit is, whilst keeping in sight how the Spirit relates to us in experience.

Love

The Spirit is love and love is important. Let me say some things about love. Love is real. I love my wife and children. I feel that God loves me. I love Jesus. How does this relate to the Holy Spirit? When I encounter the Spirit, I encounter the love of God. I experience the love of God. For Augustine, the Holy Spirit is integral to the divine love—the love of the Trinity. There is a kind of love particular to the Spirit. The love of the Spirit draws the divine persons together. The Spirit intimates and sustains the love of Father and Son. The Spirit continually enables reciprocity—mutuality—between the divine persons.[14] There is something about the Spirit that *is* love. The Spirit *is* the unity of the Father and the Son.[15] This does not mean the Spirit is merely some*thing* that holds Father and Son together. It is more that the love of the Holy Spirit is integral to the being of God. God would not be God, without the Spirit being love; without the Spirit being love in person. Not that love is unique to the Spirit. The Father loves, the Son loves, but the Spirit is foremost when we think of the love of God. When John says that "God is love,"[16] he implies in the next breath that we know the love of God because of the Spirit.[17]

It is unsurprising, therefore, that as we encounter the Spirit, we encounter God as love. It might seem indulgent that we get to bask in God's love. But this is what happens when we are in the presence of the Holy Spirit. We experience the love of God. The security, elation, and joy we associate with the best of love, we receive when encountering the Spirit. Love's definition is rooted in God; love is not something that exists apart

---

13. I am following the categorization offered by Kotsko in "Gift and Communio." I am also interacting with the text of *On the Trinity* itself. Andrew Wilson likewise highlights "gift" and "joy" in relation to the Spirit in his *Spirit and Sacrament*. His focus is more ecclesial than doctrinal. See chapters 2–3.

14. Augustine, *On the Trinity*, 15.

15. Kotsko, "Gift and Communio," 7.

16. 1 John 4:8.

17. 1 John 4:13.

from God. It is a gift of God's self; a gift of the Spirit. The nature of the divine love is that it reaches out. That is why we can experience it. The love of the Spirit is not something that God keeps to himself. Divine love, by nature, includes the ability to reach from the eternal to the temporal.[18] The love of the Spirit crosses over; it reaches over even to us. We can also say here that the same love of the Spirit, in reaching us, enables us to reach others. Love crosses the gap. The love of the Spirit draws us not only into the life of God but also to people, both similar to us and different. To want to reach out to each other is to have caught something of "who" the Spirit is.

The love of the Spirit is not merely sentimental love. It is a love that brings a radical unity of persons. Unity of persons is no easy thing. We say we value love in our society. Some even say that all we need is love. I actually agree. But when we talk about the love of the gospel—the love of the Holy Spirit—we are talking of a very particular kind of love. We are talking about a love that breaks down barriers, overcomes difference, enters the fabric of things, redeeming them and sanctifying them. The love I felt for those teenagers in Manchester was not an easy love. It was a love that made me realize something needed to be done. I had to cross over to the other side. It was a response to the healing gift of love. I could only do it because I had received something of the unifying love of the Spirit. Not that *our* love is a good example of the divine love, but when the Holy Spirit refines our love, we see it transform others; we see it reflect the love of the Spirit.

Gift

The Spirit is "gift." This assertion is critical to forming an adequate theology of the Spirit. Likewise, it is vital for an adequate charismatic theology. If the Spirit is not a gift, there is no difference between the Holy Spirit and any other Spirit. We can contrast gift with "earned." "Earned" has no place in relation to the Holy Spirit. Charismatic Christianity at its worst, forgets that the Spirit is a gift. It makes the Spirit something that needs to be whipped up and brought to bear. It makes the Spirit one who only comes when enough faith is present.

James Torrance relays the experience of talking with an exhausted Pentecostal minister. His tiredness was much to do with what he faced each Sunday: "For ten years he had been 'whipping up' himself and his congregation to live out their experience. He said 'I am weary and tired

18. Kotsko, "Gift and Communio," 8.

and have come to recognize that the center is all wrong. We feed upon Christ, the Bread of Life, not our own subjective experience."'[19] This man had clearly taken it upon himself to ensure Holy Spirit encounter happened. Eventually he came to recognize the gifted nature of the gospel, came to recognize worship as *participation* with the Spirit. This changed the pastor's ministry for good.

Seeing the gifted nature of the Spirit is fundamental to understanding the kind of Spirit we are talking about. The Spirit desires relationship. The Spirit is not interested in competing for our attention or dominating. The Spirit does not demand that we jump through certain hoops before showing up. Being spiritual is not something we just do. We are too fallen for that. It is culturally acceptable to be "Spiritual". Saying that we need the Holy Spirit is not. It smacks too much of dependency, of submission even. However, the Spirit can only be unmerited gift. We need the Spirit to restore our relationship with God because we haven't got the ability to do this ourselves. Reformed theology teaches this when it is at its best. Our approach to God has been undertaken for us. Christ has done everything required to bring us into God's presence. Being brought into God's presence is a shear act of grace.

The Spirit enables our worship and our prayer. Prayer is a response to the Spirit's invitation to take part in God's ways—a response to God's loving gift. It expresses what God is already doing with us and for us. Tom Smail states:

> As the Spirit takes the love and power of Christ with which he serves the Father and makes them ours, so also he takes the intercessory prayer of Christ in heaven and makes it ours here on earth. In the Spirit we pray Christ's perfect prayer with him. Christ prays for us before we pray for ourselves, but he keeps nothing to himself. He invites and enables us to participate.[20]

We are invited into the life of the Trinity—the life of God—as we take part with the Spirit, as we worship, and as we pray. This participation is a gift of God. Christ carries us in prayer. Prayer is thus a gift of grace in the Spirit. When we pray in the Spirit, we come by grace into the presence of the Trinity; we participate through the Spirit in the life of God.

Augustine wrestles with what it means to say the Spirit is a gift. If a gift, then it is almost as though the Spirit has been waiting around ready

---

19. Torrance, *Worship, Community*, 22–23.

20. Tom Smail, quoted in McSwain, *Movements of Grace*, 139.

to be given. It concerns him that this might imply inactivity or passivity. Likewise, if the Spirit is a gift of the Father, does that not mean the Spirit is not God in the same way as the Father? Is the Spirit merely a tool of the Father's bidding? In response to these concerns, Augustine focuses on the distinctive way the Spirit is gift. The Spirit isn't *just* given by the Father for our salvation. Yes, the Spirit enables us to commune with the Father, but the Spirit is more than this. The Spirit is *for* us. The Spirit is not just *a* gift; rather, the Spirit *is* gift. The Spirit is by nature self-giving. We might say that the Spirit's eternal activity is gifted readiness—ready for those whom God will create. It as though the Spirit is a compressed coil, ready to spring. When we encounter the Spirit, we are encountering someone whose readiness and desire for us is eternal. The Spirit's readiness for encounter is active. This applies to our experience of God. It is not upon us to create the conditions for this. God is ready. The Spirit wants to meet with us.

God the Spirit both unifies and reaches out. The Spirit shows God's activity is not only internal but also external. If we recognize that the Spirit is gift, we also recognize that the Spirit is directed outwards. When receiving the Spirit, we encounter one who has always desired us. This means we don't encounter someone who only comes in response to our faith. It is in the nature of the Spirit to move towards us creatures. This doesn't mean that we should not invite the Spirit. We can still say "Come, Holy Spirit." When I have prayed this before, there has been a tangible sense of the Spirit. The Spirit seems to be present in a way different to before we prayed. However, praying it is not what makes it happen. Prayer is more our fitting response to what has already been given. If we think about who the Spirit is, we find it is not surprising that the Spirit is so willing to be tangibly present when we say "come."

Augustine may not have been thinking of the average charismatic worship meeting when he spoke of "love" and "gift."[21] Nevertheless, these things make sense in relation to the Holy Spirit. Not least is the fact that in the charismatic movement, there is a focus on "the gifts." Again, without getting into the nature of these gifts, the point is that they are precisely that—gifts.[22] It is an important reminder to charismatics in particular that we are not doing anything special when we expect the Spirit to come.

21. Although Augustine was no cessationist.

22. Wilson talks about the gift-giving nature of God. See *Spirit and Sacrament*, 36–38. God loves to give gifts, charismatic and otherwise. God is certainly the gift giver, but our focus here is more particularly on the Spirit *as* gift. The Spirit *is* gift.

We have not unlocked the Spirit. At most, the charismatic movement recognizes what has always been true with the Spirit. That everything in the Spirit is gift. The Spirit desires to be known ever anew amongst God's people. Yes, God is doing a new thing, not least in the charismatic and Pentecostal movements, but then again, God always was.

Enjoyment

There is enjoyment in the Spirit. Hearts are lifted. There is delight, vibrancy, even fun. And so there should be. Our Christian piety shouldn't belittle these things. God's heart is one of delight in us. The activity of the Spirit can surprise, encourage or lift the veil of worry. Augustine states:

> Therefore that unspeakable conjunction of the Father and His image is not without fruition, without love, without joy. Therefore, that love, delight, felicity, or blessedness, if indeed it can be worthily expressed by any human word . . . is the Holy Spirit in the Trinity, not begotten, but the sweetness of the begetter and of the begotten, filling all creatures according to their capacity with abundant bountifulness and copiousness.[23]

If Augustine—not always recognized for his positivity—says the Spirit brings an abundance of delight, so can we! Enjoyment is an integral part of our experience, amongst other things, in the charismatic. Notice the words bountifulness and copiousness. God goes beyond the necessary. The Spirit gives more. I think we can have a fear of enjoyment. We feel it is too indulgent—too inward focused. If it was all we sort in the Christian life, then there might be a cause for concern. However, we dismiss the work of the Spirit if we do not allow for it at all.

The Spirit, through filling us, brings us image bearers into joyous bounty. Again, Augustine is not talking about the modern charismatic movement. Nevertheless, many would testify to this being how the Spirit works in their experience. There is an ecstatic joy experienced in worship and prayer. This joy builds community—builds memory. It creates stories testifying to the delight found in the presence of the Spirit. Our joy becomes fuller the more we attend to the ministry of the Spirit. And we can say we share this joy with Spirit, Son, and Father. It is not only the Spirit

---

23. Augustine, *On the Trinity*, 103.

who is about joy. Through enjoying the Spirit's presence, we become open to God's heart. We learn something about God.

Andrew Wilson notes that Jesus came spreading joy. His first miracle was turning water into wine. Wine, despite what it can do at its worst, is all about joy and merriment. So, Wilson on Jesus, "He is always sitting at the fun table, so much so that his enemies accuse him . . . of being a drunken and a glutton. That tells us something. God is happier than people think he ought to be in the circumstances."[24] Just so with Pentecost. Many thought they had had too much wine.[25] How dare they be so joyful? But the Spirit brings joy. We receive joy. Something is happening between ourselves and God. And it reflects who the Spirit is: personal, reciprocal, intimate, joyful. By focusing on our experience of the Spirit—our joy in the Spirit—we give attention to who the Spirit is. There is joy within the Godhead. God delights in us, just as he delights in his relations as Trinity.

Intimacy

Intimacy—or the propensity towards it—is a characteristic of the Spirit. Although not directly on Augustine's list, it is important. It is something I have been vying for throughout. Here, more than with anything else, the charismatic movement has caught sight of something. The Spirit is intimate. Being "in the Spirit" is intimate. And intimacy is good. There are many reasons we might shy away from intimacy, but most of us seek it. Take the intimacy and joy we find in sexual union. Such a union requires physical and emotional vulnerability. We seek these unions despite the personal risks involved. People seek them, even when they are unsure whether the feeling is mutual.

Somewhat differently, we see this in friendship and family life. There is something in our deepest relationships that reflects the intimacy and joy of the Spirit. Not that the intimacy of human relationships is a perfect picture of divine intimacy—far from it. Nevertheless, it is not surprising that intimacy is present among God's image-bearing creatures. The intimacy of the Spirit coming to us mirrors the tenderness and vulnerability of the incarnation. As Christ comes amongst us—close enough to have his feet wiped with perfume—so the Spirit becomes involved in our desires, our loves, and our passions. The Spirit being poured out on us is

24. Wilson, *Spirit and Sacrament*, 44.
25. Acts 2:13.

a vulnerable thing of God. We don't just receive an empowering force, we receive a personal encounter.

There are dangers in talk of this manner. The Spirit is not merely an intimate companion, not merely the object of our desire. As we have said, our desires need purifying. They are not reliable in themselves. We therefore relate our Spirit experience to Christ. Just as Christ is challenging and unsettling, so is the Spirit. As the Son challenges our notions of divinity by becoming human, so the Spirit does by coming in intimacy towards us. Intimacy requires vulnerability. Vulnerability is not easy. But as God's creatures we can be vulnerable with the Spirit. Yes, it is a risk; but as we take this risk, we see God is for us. We too can be vulnerable with each other knowing who the Spirit is, knowing that our vulnerability is likewise a reflection of the divine intimacy.

The Spirit, as we will see now, is the adopting one; the one who comes alongside in familial intimacy.

3

The Spirit of Adoption

A Sermon

Romans 8:14–17

[14]For all who are led by the Spirit of God are children of God. [15]For you did not receive a spirit of slavery to fall back into fear, but you have received a spirit of adoption. When we cry, "Abba! Father!" [16]it is that very Spirit bearing witness with our spirit that we are children of God, [17]and if children, then heirs, heirs of God and joint heirs with Christ—if, in fact, we suffer with him so that we may also be glorified with him.

FAMILY IS A LOVELY concept. Putting aside the potential negatives, it brings to mind notions of sharing life together, being intimate, and leaning on each other for support. We Christians talk about each other as family. So what makes us a family? The passage is clear—the Holy Spirit. The Spirit is the one who leads us together, joins us together, and keeps us together. As we look around in a gathering like this one today, we can say that we are family. We can say it because of the Spirit's ministry amongst us.

Our passage says a lot about the Holy Spirit. It begs the question, therefore, who is the Holy Spirit? The Spirit is not just a presence, an energy, or a force. The Spirit is a person. You have probably heard that said before, so what does it mean? It means that the Spirit is alive, relational, and reciprocal. The passage implies that the Spirit wants to lead people, even us. We can ask, therefore, what might it mean to "be led" by the Spirit?

"14For all who are led by the Spirit of God are children of God."

Paul says that the Spirit of God leads the children of God. He does not say "become a child of God and *then* ask for the Spirit to lead you." Being led by the Spirit comes first. Being a child of God *only* comes through being led by the Spirit. Do we want the Spirit of God to lead us? Do we want to be children of God? I hope your response is "yes please," but the shape of that child/parent relationship requires some figuring out.

For starters, the Spirit does not follow the motto "keep yourself to yourself." The Spirit is not like the neighbors on some of our streets! The Holy Spirit is not a private person. The Spirit loves us humans and wants to be in on our lives. The Spirit wants to lead us. This is good news! More than this, the Spirit wants a relationship. With the Spirit, it is always relational.

"15aFor you did not receive a spirit of slavery to fall back into fear,
but you have received a spirit of adoption."

This is a great verse for when we are in fear. But there is more to it—it has a context. It is sometimes said that they built the Roman Empire on slavery. Some early Christians would have been slaves—literal slaves. Paul has such people in mind here. These people would have existed to serve a wealthy family. Imagine being owned by someone. Imagine having everything in life decided for you. Imagine no free time, no opportunities, and no choices. Imagine that this was the course of your whole life. Imagine not expecting that to change. It is such a difficult thing to imagine because most of us have known so much freedom. There is still a great deal of slavery in the world but it is alien to the majority of us.

The gospel is contrary to slavery. Many early Christians actually set slaves free: not immediately, but it was headed that way. The New Testament book Philemon is all about this. Paul encourages Philemon to let his slave Onesimus go free. The point is, there is something about the Spirit that brings freedom: psychological freedom, emotional freedom, but also real-world freedom. This is why Paul says, "where the Spirit of the Lord is, there is freedom."[1] He is right. We feel this freedom and safety as we encounter the Spirit. For slaves, coming into freedom would only be worth it if safety and security could be guaranteed in their new setting. That is why Paul mentions fear. Slaves would have been fearful of leaving slavery. "Spirit of

---

1. 2 Cor 3:17.

fear" is literal and metaphorical. Leaving slavery is fearful whether physical slavery or psychological slavery. The stakes are high, but Paul is confident. The Spirit offers what amounts to a guarantee. When the Spirit draws us into God's family, we are safe—safe enough to leave our slavery behind.

We are not just safe, we are adopted. The Spirit is an adopter. We have received "a spirit of adoption." The Spirit fills us with the loving life of God. The Spirit causes joy to bubble up inside us. Being in a loving family feels good—is good. Our physical family circumstances vary. Some of us find it easy to talk about the comforts or joys of family life; others don't. Regardless of whether we have experienced love and acceptance, the Spirit is about our adoption, about our acceptance. The Spirit wants to confirm this adoption with people even today, whether for the first time or as a timely reminder. The Spirit wants to show you how loved you are.

When we worship and pray, we meet with the adopting Spirit. Many of us have felt something in these moments. We are supposed to. We are feeling the love of God—feeling the intimacy of the Holy Spirit. This is what charismatic Christianity has helped recover—this wonderful sense of the indwelling of the Spirit. We would do well to keep making much of this.

Adoption in the Spirit is also adoption into a community. Through the Spirit, we become part of God's community on earth—the church. Look around you—this is your new adoptive family. With all our faults, vulnerabilities, and insecurities, we make a new family home together. When we are young, we think leaving home will bring freedom. We will be able to do whatever we want whenever we want. But it is a strange freedom if we end up only living for ourselves. Freedom is no freedom if we become a slave to our own whims and desires. Our freedom only really comes in family: this new family that we are adopted in to. Freedom does not come through self-sufficiency as the world so often tells us; it comes through being led by the Spirit; it comes through community.

I remember reading Roald Dahl's classic *The BFG* with my sons.[2] You may know the story. We find out that a young girl, Sophie, was living in an orphanage. One night the BFG spotted her looking out the window at him. He could not let news of his existence get out (he was a giant, after all), so he picked her up and took her away to his cave in Giant Country. He lifted her out of her circumstances at the orphanage. Together, they left her old life behind. This was scary to begin with, but Sophie came to realize that this giant was kind and wanted to care for her. It is a lovely story.

2. Dahl, *BFG*.

Admittedly, the BFG is not a perfect image of adoption in the Spirit, but it helps illustrate the radical difference between what we are brought out of and what we come into.

But adoption is not just something done unto. In the Spirit, God wants to collaborate with us—wants us as co-builders. In the Spirit, we are enabled to take part in what God is doing in the world. The BFG is so wonderful because it is an adventure. The BFG and Sophie are doing something risky and exciting together. The tenderness with which he treats Sophie is beautiful—this big, powerful giant and this vulnerable young girl. Sophie gets to ride along in his ear; she gets to go dream catching with him; she even persuades the BFG to get rid of the child-eating giants. Hanging out with the Holy Spirit is an adventure. We adopted children get to take part in exciting and unpredictable exploits that will mark us for the rest of our lives.

> "15b*When we cry, "Abba! Father!"* 16*it is that very Spirit bearing witness with our spirit that we are children of God,"*

Adoption creates a new family dynamic. This happens when the Spirit adopts us. Because the Spirit is at work in us, we can call God the Father "our Father." We can even call God "Abba." Abba is an intimate word. However we translate it (Daddy, Papa, Father), the relationship that the Spirit brings us into is intimate.[3] The Father is eternally the Father by nature. He is the Father of everyone. But when the Spirit enables our adoption, he becomes *our* Father—hence, Abba. We are not just empowered by the Spirit—we become intimate family.

Coming into a new family has its difficulties. It is difficult to become a Christian. With families, we are at our most vulnerable. We cannot shield ourselves from them; we share so much with them. In most of our relationships, it takes a while for defenses to come down. But when coming into the family of God, the difficulty lies only with us. The Spirit is not wary of us; the Spirit is not cautious with us. It's amazing: God desires, more than anything else, a family relationship with you and I.

---

3. Joachim Jeremias memorably suggested that Abba was a "children's word, used in everyday talk." This led to the popular notion that it means "daddy." See Jeremias, *Proclamation of Jesus*, 67. Suffice to say, not everyone agrees.

"17And if children, then heirs, heirs of God and joint heirs with Christ—
if, in fact, we suffer with him so that we may also be glorified with him."

Family ties were important in the world of the New Testament. They still are, particularly in some cultures. Families extended well beyond the nuclear family. Patronage, the privilege that comes through being part of a family, was an especially big deal: Your identity, your status, and your security. It was difficult to break with your patronage. If you were an heir, you had full use of the privileges available, so abandoning family would be anathema. You would be cut off from the community, and it would be unlikely that you would ever be welcomed back. It rarely happened by choice.

The Christian community's claim to have a new patron was radical. To many, it was objectionable. It was risky for the early Christians to say they had a new Lord, particularly when this Lord was someone who underwent a shameful death on a cross. Paul's teaching is that the Spirit enables a new patronage. If we are in Christ, we are joint heirs with him. The Spirit draws us to our new patron—Abba Father. Our old patronage has gone. If we are to know the Spirit, if we are to experience the power, transformation, and joy of the Spirit, we must put our former patronage to one side. That is still the case today. It still has a cost, whoever we are. But let me tell you that it is worth it.

As the community of Christ, we can put any privilege that our upbringings may or may not have given us to one side. Most of us will not leave our actual families behind—in most cases, it would be wrong to. After all, family is a gift from God. I, for one, enjoy real closeness with my family. But seeing our blood family as more important than God's family is not compatible with the gospel. Are you proud of your family roots? Don't be.

Likewise, if our background or education give us rights and privileges, we shouldn't see this as a good thing. If our gender, ethnicity, or sexuality give us some kind of security, then our values may need questioning. This includes being middle class: middle class does not exist in God's family. Likewise, being working class. In this new family, status is reset. We are all on an equal footing. The Spirit will not allow high or low status in the new family. If we make anything a reason not to relate to a fellow family member, we dishonor the Spirit, the very one who brought us into the community.

When we come together to worship, it can take us a while to get into it. The pressures of the week, or even the day, still occupy our thoughts. Our family tie to the world still wants to take hold of us. Our former patronage draws us back to the security it provided. We become consumed with our worries: money; security; fitting in. These things make it difficult for us to readjust as we come back to our true community—make it difficult to come into the presence of God. But it is not the Spirit who puts up these barriers. The Spirit wants us in the presence of the Father. We must put these things to one side if we are to commune with the Spirit, if we are to cry Abba Father. We have nothing to fear. Worship is the place in which we should feel most at home. It is our family gathering with each other and with the Spirit.

There is more to the work of the Spirit than *our* adoption. There is more to being an heir than being able to call God "our Father." We don't just inherit the fortune; we take on responsibility for the house, for the land. We take on responsibility for God's creation. In the ancient world, inheritance wasn't just about getting something; it was also about taking responsibility *for* something. We seem to have lost this idea. I had several farming friends growing up, some of whom knew real financial hardship. As young teenagers, they already worked the farm, already took responsibility for the family business. As soon as the Spirit leads us into adoption, we too take on the family business. We become adopters.

But we cannot take on the business without going through some hardship. That is why Paul says we should know "the sharing of his sufferings."[4] Christ's hardship was very particular. His cost was unique. We cannot emulate it. But we *are* called to share that cost. If we are co-heirs with Christ, then we are to enter his suffering. Being an heir means becoming responsible for the world as Christ was. And becoming responsible for the world means taking part in the world's suffering. In this way we understand the heart of the Spirit; understand what it means to be poured out for all people.

We cannot read this passage and conclude the Spirit is inward-looking. The Spirit always reaches out. If we are in the Spirit, we will also have this inclination. The Spirit wants to fill every space with the love of God. In verse 22, Paul talks about creation "groaning as in the pains of childbirth." The Spirit who wants to give birth also wants to fill the earth. That is why we, as adopted children, must catch the adopting heart of the Spirit. When the Spirit cries within us "Abba Father," we also cry out for the world. We cry out for all to become part of the family.

If we get the Spirit—get that the Spirit adopts—we likewise understand that adoption doesn't end with us. The world is groaning for adoption and the good news is that the adopter is ready and with us. The church is the

4. Phil 3:10.

adopted community of God. We carry the presence of the Holy Spirit. To be a joint heir with Christ means to go into the world and make disciples of all nations. This is the vision for God's big family. We are just the firstfruits of the harvest—the start of God's kingdom project, not the end. That is why we should reach the unreached; why we should love the unlovable, the vulnerable, the broken; why we should pray for people in our workplaces, in our neighborhoods, and in our streets.

We cannot convert people to Christianity. We can show people what adoption in the Spirit looks like—what it is like to be a Spirit-filled community. We can show people what it is like to be an heir with Christ, what it is like to have Abba as our Father. Who will you adopt today?

Conclusion

SPIRIT EXPERIENCE HAS MUCH to do with theology. A theology of the Spirit benefits greatly from talking about experience—from a consideration of the depth of our encounter with the Spirit. This does not go against classical ways of talking about the Spirit. The Spirit has always enabled encounter and in doing so given an understanding of the character of God. The character of the Spirit is love, joy, and vitally, gift. If we lose sight of the Spirit as gift we miss the necessity of grace. If we lose sight of our need for grace, we lose the Spirit. What we experience in Spirit encounter reinforces and beautifies what we already know of the Spirit—that the Spirit enables our adoption and reconciliation with God.

My experiences of the Spirit have impacted how I see God. They act as confirmation that I am loved by God. It is something that I feel each moment in communion with the Spirit. It is difficult to say this. My concern is that it sounds all too subjective, that it doesn't sound clever enough. But that is part of the point. Spirit encounter undoes our need to sound clever. Yes, it is unsettling, giving our emotions over to something we cannot see. However, encounter with the Spirit is like nothing else. It is something to continue to yearn for; something to continue being Christian for.

The Spirit desires intimacy with the community. Our experience testifies to this. But there are things to watch out for, not least the temptation to think that the Spirit must act in a particular way, according to our bidding. The Spirit is free to blow any which way. Crucial, is the relation of Christ and Spirit. The Spirit never acts in contradiction to Jesus. Staying focused on Christ means we do not run away with our thoughts. What we experience in the Spirit is filtered through what we know of Christ in the flesh, what we know of him from Scripture. The appeal of Christ is one with the appeal of the Spirit.

There is more to the Spirit than our individual experiences. Likewise, the Spirit is not limited to our communal experiences as the visible people of God. The Spirit is the Spirit of the whole earth as adopter and reconciler. To be in the Spirit is to be an adopter because in being so we catch something of being poured out for others. And thus, the Spirit not only motivates our understanding of the church, but our understanding of God's action throughout the earth. The Spirit helps us see what God is up to, what God wants, today.

Part 3

Knowing God

Introduction

ALBERT SCHWEITZER ONCE SAID that Jesus "comes to us as one unknown."[1] Was he right? He didn't mean we can't know anything about Jesus. Christ, though coming in mystery, is not opaque. So too with God, said Schweitzer. He conceded that through our experience of the world, we gain *some* knowledge of God's mystery. But that is all. So can we know Christ? Can God be known? Is God known, but unknown? If known, even in part, then what? Despite the difficulties associated with saying that God can be known, we can contend for more than Schweitzer. I think God wants to be known and if God wants to be known, we can know God. To say otherwise is to limit God—is to say that God is not free to be who he might want to be. I also think it is okay to say that when we feel as though we are knowing God, we just might be.

Experience is important here again. Knowing, in no small part, is experienced, felt, lived. My experience involves the *feeling* of knowing God. This would be an empty assertion if it were not accounted for in relation to Christ and Spirit. But that has been our business so far. Knowledge relates to the incarnation of the Word; to Christ's coming close. It also relates to the receiving of the Spirit; to encountering the vibrant life of the Spirit. In discussing the knowledge of God, as much as anywhere, my experience relates also to wrestling with the thoughts of theologians. Here, particularly, we will attend to theologians off the beaten track in terms of my background. We will consider seriously some fruitful concepts identified by these theologians.

1. Schweitzer, *Historical Jesus*, 401.

79

Can we *fully* know God? I will not contend for that, but will aim to show why we can hope to know God truly, really and meaningfully. Theologians have spoken of God's communicable and incommunicable attributes. We can know God through certain communicable attributes, whereas God's incommunicable attributes are at most only partly comprehendible.[2] Maybe when we feel as though we are getting to know God, it is God's communicable attributes we are getting to know. It is a neat way of drawing a distinction—allowing for some knowledge whilst acknowledging the problem of transcendence. However, it is a questionable distinction. I don't think God needs protecting behind so-called incommunicable attributes. God's self-communication requires no false limit. This marks one of the turns away from the teachings of my tradition. Evangelical theologies often start with God's attributes and then move to protect them. God doesn't need protecting. What has taught me this is the other side of my theological formation—the charismatic. Through what is taking place in charismatic encounter, we see that God is a communicating God; a God who is doing the very opposite to holding things back behind the veil.

So where does knowledge arise? It could arise from nature. It could come when we recognize the hand of the creator in the world. We call this natural theology. I teach a unit called "The knowledge of God" to sixteen-year-olds. It is an interesting thing to consider with a group of teenagers with various views on the existence of God, including atheism, various types of theism, and indifference! We compare natural theology with revealed theology. Revealed theology focusses on God's self-revelation: through Scripture, through Christ or through religious experience. It takes the tack that we cannot know God unless God chooses to be known, unless God chooses to self-reveal. The students find it difficult to get the essence of the two approaches. Mostly, they struggle to see *why* it matters. Without getting into it too much, my interest is more in revealed theology. I must acknowledge that this only makes sense from the context of my Christian faith. I cannot convince someone that this approach is neutrally useful. The thing is, I am not asking whether we can know *about* God. When I pose the question, "can we know God?" I am asking whether we can know God *personally*.

I have always felt known by God. I also feel I know God. The first is easy to say, the second not so. To return to the motivations for being Christian, I can add that it is because I believe God wants to be known. If I were

2. Wayne Grudem's, *Systematic Theology*, for example, has separate chapters on God's "Incommunicable Attributes" and "Communicable Attributes," 156–225.

to say this to my colleagues and my students, they may well think I had tipped over the edge into absurdity. I am aware of the presumption of my claim. It is a cautious claim, but I still make it. I have already outlined some problems in saying we know God. There is the danger that we imply that God is just an extension of our wishes and desires or the danger of implying that we can possess God. Despite these problems, I still believe God wants to be known—even today—even this moment.

Why do I insist on the knowledge of God? When I enter intimate relations, I gain a sense that knowledge is taking place. As said, this is "personal" knowledge. It is more than knowledge *about* a person—what they look like, what their preferences are, etc. This point is encapsulated by the philosopher Martin Buber. He says that when we know a person well, we know them more as a "you" than an "it."[3] Our knowledge of someone we know well comes through reciprocity. It is subject to subject, rather than subject to object. When I know someone, I don't know them as an object, I actually know them. I know them in a way that means I let them into my life. We are more vulnerable with those we know well. In fact, to get to know people well, we need to be vulnerable with them. People are more than "its," more than objects. I have this same sense when I consider relating to God. When speaking about God, I am not talking about an object, but a being in relationship.

There are several places where relating takes place: in prayer and worship; through charismatic encounter with the Spirit; through breaking bread. These are instances of great intimacy and what seem to be great willingness on God's part. There is a risk in this talk because it implies that God and I connect relationally with no barriers—no limits. Again, Christology can protect us from this risk. I measure the knowledge taking place by grounding it in Scripture and Christ. Were we not to have Christ's incarnation and were we not to have Scripture, we would only have our experience; we would only have our desires. This is what I aimed to establish in the previous part. The point is, we are not left without God in our lives. Scripture shows that we can hope for personal relationship.

The God of Scripture, the God of Jesus Christ, has given himself to be known. The way God is, includes *wanting* to be known. Scripture is very clear about this. The writer to the Hebrews, for example, says "but in these last days he has spoken to us by a Son, whom he appointed heir of

---

3. Or, more accurately, we know them more as a "Thou" than an "It." See Buber, *I and Thou*, 53–60.

all things, through whom he also created the worlds. He is the reflection of God's glory and the exact imprint of God's very being."[4] In Christ, God speaks himself to us. God doesn't just speak through the Son as if through a mouthpiece; the Son is the coming of God, the making known of God, God in person. The Son comes as one to be known.

C. S. Lewis said of Aslan, the beloved central character of his Chronicles of Narnia, that he is "Not like a *tame* lion."[5] But there is no implication that Aslan was holding back: that Lucy, Susan, Edmund, and Peter were not getting the real deal with Aslan. The relation of intimacy could not be more striking; otherwise Lucy could not have buried her head in his mane; would not have been able to ride on his back.[6] Yes, God is not tame. The accounts of God's dealings with his people in the Hebrew Scriptures testify to this. More than once God's face is hidden from his people.[7] The followers of Jesus knew it. Jesus was unsettling to be around and certainly not predictable. But by saying not tame, I don't mean distant or invulnerable. We may not want to cast God in overly familiar terms, but this does not amount to God's reticence in relating to us. Even when God hides his face, it is a relational event. Everything points to his existing for us, to a propensity for relationship, a willingness to be known. We should avoid saying anything that results in implying that God becomes compromised by his association with us. Yet, on God's part, his tender mercy looks very much like coming towards us—to taking our form and being found amongst us.

4. Hebrews 1:2–3a
5. See Lewis, *The Lion, the Witch*, 166.
6. Lewis, *The Lion, the Witch*, 149.
7. Deuteronomy 32:20; Micah 3:4; Ezekiel 39:23, etc.

1

Free to be Known

God's Freedom and Love

DURING MY FIRST YEAR at theological college, our lecturer warned us: "Beware of saying that God *must* act in a particular way." My first reaction was that God cannot contradict his nature, so surely there are things he must do. But slowly, I saw that she was right. And believing this does something to us. If we construct systems that result in us saying what God must be like, we are on shaky ground. It is easy to let it happen. We can often say things like "God must be faithful to his promises" or "God cannot allow sin in his presence." It may be that everything points to the fact that these things *are* true of God. There is an evangelical tendency, in wanting to affirm truths about God, to insist that God must do things. But it is a questionable tendency. I don't think such statements should be made into imperatives, particularly when they become impositions on God. We do not get to hold God to account.

To illustrate the point, we can recall the story of the Lord appearing to Moses through the flames of the bush. God is going to ask Moses to do something. But before he received his task, God showed Moses who he was: "I am the God of your father, the God of Abraham, the God of Isaac, and the God of Jacob."[1] Moses was reminded of God's record of covenant faithfulness. God is faithful to his word. Whatever God would ask him to do, Moses could trust God. God spoke again: "I have seen the misery of my people who are in Egypt." Moses could also trust God, knowing that he cares. God hadn't forgotten his people; God would not abandon them. Nevertheless, Moses was concerned about how the Israelites would respond,

1. For what follows, see Exod 3:1–12.

83

let alone the Egyptians. How would they know who this God was? Moses received no long explanation; no proof. He simply heard, "I am who I am." Why? Because as much as God's track record relates to who he is, God is primarily who God is.

God's track record is important without being a limitation. It doesn't control him. God does not *have* to act in a certain way. God acts according to who he is, according to his will, according to his love, not out of fear of being inconsistent with what he has done before. Will God act consistently? Yes. Does God have to? No. That is why he says "I am who I am." God is who God is, not who we say he must be.

To avoid saying "God must" we might say that "God is free." But what do we mean by "free"? One way we use the word today is to say "free from": free from sugar; free from artificial flavorings; carbon free (or neutral). We can ask now, is this freedom? Being free *from* implies being unconditioned. Most of us would want to say this of God. We cannot affect or condition God. Indeed, this is the classic Augustinian view of God's freedom. Katherine Sonderegger summarizes it thus: Freedom is "enshrined and *constituted* by the exercise of the Will, to execute or to refrain" or as "doing what one wills."[2] Freedom, in other words, is the power to act voluntarily. On this reckoning, God alone can act in complete freedom because God alone is unconditioned. God alone can say something according to his will and know for sure it will happen.

But is this all we want to say for freedom? Sonderegger thinks not. Freedom might be the power to do as one wills, but freedom is more importantly being who one is. God is free because God is who he is.[3] Thus, God's freedom might include wanting to be known. This is freedom for God because it relates to who God is. If we are too quick to point out the dangers in saying that God might be knowable, then we place limits upon God; we define the terms for God. We need not fear that God's freedom is at stake if God wants to be known. This is one of the central features of my argument. It applies to what we have said about both Son and Spirit. The Son is the reality of God for us and with us. This means very little if it is not God that we are knowing in the Son—if it is merely a human representation of God. In getting to know Jesus, I find I am getting to know God. Just so, with our experience of the Spirit. If it is God's will to relate to us intimately, then we cannot say that to do so would jeopardize God's freedom. And therein

2. Sonderegger, *Doctrine of God*, 310.
3. Sonderegger, *Doctrine of God*, 318.

lies the strength of the argument: God's freedom includes the freedom to be known and in being known not cease to be free.

The nature of God's freedom is that God can communicate himself to us, commune with us, be involved in the human situation, enter into our lives, be intimate with us, and still be God; still be who God is. We can thus talk about both God's freedom *and* God's entering our situation. Dietrich Bonhoeffer states that God's freedom is not so much "freedom from" as it is "freedom for."[4] This encapsulates what I have been arguing for. God's freedom is not a distant freedom; God is not free through disassociation with us. God is free *for* us and *with* us. And this is freedom. If freedom cannot be freedom *for*, then it is not freedom.

Bonhoeffer does not stop there. He provocatively states that God is not only free *for* us but that this freedom is manifest in God's being "bound" to us. God binds himself to us—it is that personal. And Bonhoeffer insists that God binds himself freely. God does not lose himself in coming to us. Put more fully,

> In revelation it is not so much a question of the freedom of God— eternally remaining within the divine self, aseity—on the other side of revelation, as it is of God's coming out of God's own self in revelation. It is a matter of God's *given* Word, the covenant in which God is bound by God's own action. It is a question of the freedom of God, which finds its strongest evidence precisely in that God freely chose to be bound to historical human beings and to be placed at the disposal of human being. God is free not from human beings but for them. Christ is the word of God's freedom. God *is* present, that is, not in eternal nonobjectivity but—to put it quite provisionally for now—'haveable', graspable in the Word within the church.[5]

Some might be uncomfortable with such claims. "Bound" appears to contradict freedom. It makes it sound like God is not in control, that God has given up his rights. But what if this is what God wants? What if God remains God in being bound to us? What if God is being most himself—most free—when being bound? One of my defining realizations is that we have somehow convinced ourselves that we honor God more if we imagine him free from restraint. But we must at least allow the possibility that, in being yoked to us, God can still be God—still be free.

4. Bonhoeffer, *Act and Being*, 87.
5. Bonhoeffer, *Act and Being*, 91.

Acknowledging the *for us* nature of God is surely central to Christian faith. That God is bound to us and is therefore "haveable" is also a claim I want to make with Bonhoeffer. It is a bold one. It means that who God is, links to how God relates to us. God's nature is wrapped up in God's relation to us. Does this imply a blurring of the line between ourselves and God? I don't think so. In binding himself to us, God is acting according to himself. We have every reason to say that it is God's decision—God's desire—to be known. If God wants to be known, to be "haveable," to be bound to us, who are we to say otherwise? None of this means God *must* do this, more that God *has* done this. When we look at the incarnation of the Word and when we receive the work of the Spirit in us, we see that it has already happened. God is being haveable. Likewise, it is not just something that did happen, it is happening now.

Critically, God's binding is not something enacted by us. We haven't got it within us to grasp God. That God is graspable is to do with him. God chooses to be known. Saying God is bound need not contradict God's freedom if it is willed by God—chosen by God. God binding himself to us is not done in response to our need, it is done according to God's free action—God's eternal intention.

What this means for us is huge. We couldn't hope for more from God. God has bound himself to us. We can see it in Scripture—it has always been going on. God does not just create a world, create a people, and then leave. He enters a covenant, accommodates himself to the flesh, allows our prayers to reach him and communes with us by the Spirit. And all this flows from God's bias towards relationship—towards friendship. It is God being most truly himself, not because he has to be, but because he is, because he wants to be. The freedom bit, though, is vital. It means that God is not a victim of his own choosing. God embraces us, but we do not coerce God; we are not the ones in the driving seat setting the agenda. God's love for us is not dependent upon our love for God. This is why it is free love—why God can be bound to us without ceasing to be God.

Knowing Redeemed

Scripture speaks of a self-revealing God. Yes, there is a problem at our end, but it doesn't follow that there is a problem at God's end. We don't have the capacity to comprehend God fully. In fact, our brokenness and sinfulness have a devastating effect on our ability to know God, but that need not imply reticence on God's part. We cannot hide behind the claim that God is mystery, hoping this will guarantee God's freedom. God's freedom surely relates more to how he acts towards us—how God self-reveals. And God has revealed himself, not just as God, but as redeemer and friend. God's revelation is personal. Knowledge of God is personal because God is personal. I think we can have confidence when we say that we *feel* we know God. Thus, we should not be surprised that our knowledge relates to our feelings.

God not only wants to be known, but in his love for us, heals our brokenness. God acts towards us in a way that also heals our misapprehension of him. Our redemption gives us right standing before God—justification—but also more: it redeems our vision. God comes clearer into view as we receive salvation. Christ our Savior is God himself. Christ is both our salvation and our means of recognizing the reality of God, the love of God, and the knowledge of God. Focusing on Christ as the revelation of God is so powerful, because in him we not only see who God is, but find that our blurred vision is restored, healed, and made good. Salvation and revelation come together in Christ.

If I didn't feel as though I knew God at all, then I would have reason not to be a Christian. This sounds awful; it sounds as though I think we have the right to know God, as though if God had nothing to do with me then I couldn't believe in this God. But I can in fact say this, because of who God is. I have found a God who wants to be known. When praying, when contemplating Jesus, when experiencing the Holy Spirit, when reading the Scriptures; when I do each of these things, it is not to honor an unknown God. I do so to commune with God. Sure, I desire this but that doesn't make it any less real. What's more, I see too that it is what God desires.

I don't want to lose sight of the fact that we can recognize God because he has freed us to do so. God's atoning and reconciling work has liberated us. This changes more than our status; it transforms our vision. And this frees me to worship God, to love God, to want to bring honor to God. Our language of worship can imply that our motivation must be to honor God; that worship is not about our needs. I am sure this is as it should be. If we did anything else, it would not be worship. But we cannot insist that God follows suit, that God must seek his own honor. Despite our best intentions to honor God, maybe we sometimes misunderstand.

I used to lead the singing bit of Sunday worship. The school of thought at the time was that the first three songs should be upward focused. In other words, they should be declaratory songs, focused on the honoring of God.

It was a good idea and remains a common approach. It means our attention is directed towards God, not on the things of the week, or our own concerns. And it sometimes works. We wake up from our slumber. We recognize what and who we are gathered together for. It is a sign of evangelical commitment. But if God's reason for being there is us, hadn't we better at least recognize that in our worship? We come to worship God, not because God needs building up, but because God has set his heart upon us; has saved us; has made himself known. We could start our singing by recalling his movement towards us and by acknowledging our need of him for our salvation. I think we would do well to make such a change in emphasis. Likewise, our worship could recognize God's presence amongst us in the moment; God's being for us now. Of course, we should declare who God is; but who we know God to be is directly linked to who he is for us.

Maybe God's focus has been us all along. God might expect to be glorified; it is no less than he deserves. It might even be, as the Westminster Confession would have it, that our chief end is to glorify God. But through and through, God cares for us. We are God's focus; his desire is for us. John Piper says that God seeks us, moves towards us, for his own glorification. "The bedrock of Christian hedonism [Piper's particular project] is not God's allegiance to us, but to Himself."[6] Piper is keen to enjoy, to desire God. And the fact that God is glorified when we enjoy him means that we have permission to do so. Great; I have been saying this all along. But again, I want to claim more for what God is doing. Piper is satisfied to say of God that "He must be for Himself if He is to be for others."[7] Yes, but why place his self-glorification first? I would say that his movement towards us is *not* driven by his need to be glorified. It is born out of love. He wants *us*. This might result in his glorification, but I don't see the need to claim this for God's motivation.

And thus, God wants to be known by us. God knows that this is good for us. That is the evangelical reality of the situation. In this sense, God is more like the mother whose interest is her children than the patriarchal dictator whose interest is his own glory. Our end might be to glorify God, but God's end seems to be the love and salvation of us beloved children.

At the center of worship for many churches is the Lord's Supper, the Eucharist, Holy Communion. Communion is not so much an act of exaltation as an act of receipt. In the bread and the wine, God has come to us.

6. Piper, *Desiring God*, 31.
7. Piper, *Desiring God*, 45.

God comes to be known in the moment of receipt. Through the incarnation and the sacrament of the Word, we recognize God's desire for us. The center of worship here is God's loving kindness, God's movement towards us, as much as our exaltation of God. The focus of communion is redemption. This should provide a picture for the rest of our worship. As we sing, we are thankful recipients. Our words tell, not only of who God is in himself, but of what God has done and is doing amongst us right now.

Known Truly, not Exhaustively

I am not arguing for an unbounded or absolute knowledge of God. Nor that we know God in the same way that God knows us. It is helpful to distinguish between knowing God "truly" and knowing God "exhaustively."[8] It is knowing God "truly" that I am vying for. We know God "truly" because God wants to be known. God is not hoodwinking us when he reveals himself in the Son or through the Spirit. We are not getting God "lite." God is to us as God is. The eternal will of the Son to become incarnate, for example, is for us and for our salvation, but likewise is as an act of self-expression on God's part. God is expressing his heart for us. So as much as the incarnation is an act of grace and an act of rescue, it is also God being himself. Through the incarnation, we know God being God. But this does not mean we know God "exhaustively." Even with Christ, there is more to know than we know now. Although we have here God in reality, God in truth, God in flesh, God in our language, it doesn't mean that in Christ we know God exhaustively.

We can attend to this point further by considering the doctrine of divine accommodation. The Son of God assumes the form of a human—Jesus. God accommodates himself to our form. Here we have an act of love, an act of mercy, and an act that enables us to comprehend. But we could be in danger of making it sound as though God doesn't give himself as he really is, instead giving himself in accessible mode so our minds are not too blown. That would not do. John Calvin, although a great advocate of the doctrine of accommodation, knows it can go too far, knows that it can miss the point. A simple example illustrates the point. Sometimes it is said that the Gospels are more suitable for children or young Christians than for mature believers. The Jesus of the Gospels reveals God in childlike language, whereas the letters of Paul give us a grown-up understanding of God. For

8. See Dawson, *Introduction to Torrance*, 77. Dawson refers to Thomas Torrance but acknowledges other theologians have made the same distinction.

Calvin, this would be unacceptable. The point for him is that "God is comprehended in Christ alone."[9] In other words, God is not comprehended properly elsewhere.

Accommodation is not just about God condescending to our level, it is about directing our vision towards Christ—directing our vision to where God is. Jesus Christ is the person in whom we see God. The incomprehensibility of God becomes known in him, because the reality of God *is* in him. It is a point I have made throughout. But if we speak of accommodation wrongly it can sound as though we are only given *something* of God rather than everything. So how much of God do we get in the incarnation?

Despite Calvin's remarks on the potential for misunderstanding accommodation, he thinks there is more to the Son than we see in Jesus. The Word is not limited to incarnation in the flesh. Hence, "although the boundless essence of the Word was united with human nature into one person, we have no idea of any enclosing. The Son of God descended miraculously from heaven, yet without abandoning heaven."[10] The ministry of Jesus in the first century is not confined to Palestine. Calvin is not saying we don't get the real deal in the Son—we do, but even in the flesh, there is still a reality of the Son outside of the flesh.[11] The Son doesn't get squished into the flesh. We see the Son in person, and in our form, but not in entirety. Just as the Son had eternally existed outside the flesh, so he continues to do so even as he is in the flesh. What Calvin is doing is saying we should not make too much out of the potential of the flesh. The flesh is incapable of holding the divine nature in completeness.[12] I agree with Calvin that we do not have the capacity to contain God. But what this can imply is that there is a bit of the Son beyond and above comprehension, as though God is holding something back. This implies that there remains an unknowing in relation to the fullness of the divine Son.

Calvin is prioritizing God's freedom. He is also concerned not to make too much of the potential of human nature. However, we can claim more for Christ in the flesh. Surely, if God wills it, the Son can come fully in the flesh. Surely it is within God's creative ability to do this. We needn't protect

9. Calvin, *Institutes*, 298.

10. Calvin, *Institutes*, 414.

11. The so called "extra calvinisticum." See recently, Williams, *Christ the Heart*, 152–53.

12. This is referred to thus: "Finitum non capax infiniti," meaning, "The finite is not capable of the infinite." See Williams, *Christ the Heart*, 153. I agree, but would add that the infinite *is* capable of becoming wholly finite.

God from an association with us. Again, this points to the kind of God that I know him to be. A communicative, personal God; a God who does not hold back in self-protection. We need not protect God. We see that God wants to give everything to us. That is the pattern of creation, of covenant, of redemption. What is revealed in Scripture is a movement towards, not a movement away.

To clarify, I am not claiming perfect knowledge on our part. It is not out of a high view of human nature that I am persuaded that in Christ we have a proper picture of God. Rather, I am claiming perfect willingness and love on God's part. If God wants to be revealed in the flesh, God can be revealed in the flesh. And, I am not saying that God *has* to do this. Rather, God *has* done this. When Jesus says, "Whoever has seen me has seen the Father,"[13] he means more than a bit. At the very least, he means that, in seeing him, we have *truly* seen the Father. Without seeing Jesus, we would be without sight of God, or at least we would have disastrously blurred vision. We are lost without God, but have God when we have Jesus Christ. God's coming to us in Christ is an act of condescension, mercy, and rescue—an act of grace. But it is God being himself—doing what God does. I think we can say that in Jesus we have the whole Son.

There is mystery here. I don't have the requisite framework to understand everything there is to know about the incarnate Word. *My* nature is not human and divine! I cannot know what it is to have my nature conjoined with the divine nature. And therefore, although Christ is in every regard the making known of God to us, it is beyond me to master this. And the more I get to know Christ, the more I realize there is to know. It is not wholly dissimilar to the way in which we get to know our loved ones. There is always more; not necessarily more information, but more. Those we know the best can still surprise us. Our understanding of them is still growing. Just so with Christ—with God. But this doesn't amount to a shielding. There is no sense whereby we don't get his true self.

There is more to the Son than a humanity on a par with ours—more to Christ than there is to us. However, God enables our participation with him so that we even get to know something of what it is like to be joined to the Godhead. Our participation is not the same as Christ's participation with Father and Spirit, but it is a genuine participation nonetheless. Christian Kettler notes: "If God is able to become human, is he not able to reveal who he truly is, not simply a "part" of God or our impressions of God? The

13. John 14:9.

personal nature of the intimacy between the Father and the Son is what we partake in through the Holy Spirit. What we participate in is no less than a relationship, since we are adopted as sons and daughters (Gal 4:5)."[14] It is intimate and personal, and in being so is a relationship that gives us more than just an indication of what it is like to participate in the life of God. As adopted daughters and sons, our knowledge is very much real.

The children I teach want knowledge. Their personal level of interest in the content of theology varies, but they recognize the need to know stuff in order to succeed in their exams. For all my protestations that understanding faith requires more than "head knowledge," they remain unconvinced. But this is the point—in the Christian community we don't just want knowledge "about" God. We are not after passing an exam on God. Our desire is for more. Our interest is in getting to know God in the present. If knowledge of God is not personal, if it is not a relationship, if it is only information about some distant creator, then it is deeply dissatisfying. Not only this, but it misrepresents who God is in revelation. The God we desire in our deepest thoughts turns out to be the God who invites us to take part in his life.

Alexander Jensen makes a similar point by distinguishing between the "who" and the "what" of God. "Who" God is *can* be known, but this doesn't mean we know everything about "what" God is. The "who" is revealed through God's way of being towards us.[15] We really get God: through salvation in Christ; through baptism and the Lord's Supper; through the witness of Scripture; through encountering the Spirit. In these ways, we receive something of the "who." We might not receive everything that God is, but a genuine person-to-person encounter is ours. God is being known in such encounters. They might also involve mystery. Certainly, we don't come away in full understanding of the one we have encountered; nevertheless, personal knowledge is taking place.

I agree with Jensen's distinction: we know "who" God is in Christ and through the Spirit. As we have said, with the Spirit in particular, we know more than a presence or a force. When we encounter the Spirit in charismatic worship, we don't build up our head knowledge, we develop a relationship. Here, as much as anywhere, maybe even more than anywhere, I feel as though I am getting to know God personally. This doesn't mean that I am in full possession of the moment. There is some mystery—some

14. Kettler, *God Who Believes*, 94–95.
15. Jensen, *Divine Providence*, 25–26.

implication that there is more to know. Indeed, I am happier to allow for the place of mystery in the question of *what* God is. As I encounter the Spirit, the whole range of what God is does not open up to me. For this reason, we can say yes to mystery. But I don't want to hold back from saying *who* God is, because that doesn't equate with how God is with us. God has not held back. To be coy at this point would be to place a false limit on God's freedom to be known.

The Christian would have little to say about God if they could not say they *know* God. As Ludwig Wittgenstein enigmatically stated, "What we cannot speak about we must pass over in silence."[16] Well yes, but the point is, Christians are rarely silent about God. Even if we take an apophatic approach, we are not wholly silent. If we don't *know* God, then we cannot say anything about God. Again, by "know," I mean know personally. As Barth puts it: "everything heard in the Church would have no Subject and would be left in the air like an empty sound."[17] If God has not revealed himself to us, then we have no adequate impression of God at all. What we say in church, what we sing in worship, what we read in Scripture is not an empty sound. It is full, real, and personal. We Christians say things about God. We say them for a reason—because of the kind of God we are talking about—a God who would want us to talk about him, a God who wants to be known by us.

This is evangelical theology in its most proper sense. God can be known. We know the dangers of being too confident about our knowledge. Not least is the pitfall of fashioning God in our own image—of making God too familiar—of claiming God for our way of seeing things. Nevertheless, says Barth, "true knowledge of God is not and cannot be attacked; it is without anxiety and without doubt."[18] We can speak about God confidently because we have been given every reason to be confident. Yes, there are constraints, but they shouldn't make us shrink back. By saying that God can be known, we are not saying that our knowledge of God is automatic, wholly trustworthy, or perfect. Our knowledge needs sanctifying. It needs conforming to how God chooses to be known. But because God has revealed himself through his Word—through Christ—we can have every confidence. Knowing has a concrete ground—Jesus. And therefore, we have more than a feeling, we have a sure hope that we have caught something of God.

16. Wittgenstein, *Tractatus*, 89.
17. Barth, *CD* 2/1.3–4.
18. Barth *CD* 2/1.7.

Events of Knowing

I agree with Barth that our knowledge of God only comes through God's self-revelation. God reveals God. I also agree that our knowledge should not be *reduced* to feeling. However, knowledge *is* something we feel. Knowing is emotional as much as it is rational. Knowing something feels like something. We need not see this as an insurmountable problem. The concrete ground of our feeling—our knowing—is the Word; is the Son incarnate. When we feel as though we know God, we do so as recipients, witnesses, and beneficiaries of the incarnation—as those who have somewhere to locate that knowing. We can check our feelings against Christ and Scripture.

There can be no blurring of the line between God and ourselves. God is not us; we are not God. God comes to us as himself and does not lose himself in us. God's objectivity is uncompromised through association with us. God remains God even in becoming known. Similarly, we don't cease to be human as we come to know God. We don't become divine. But we are given access to God in Christ and through the Holy Spirit. God is accessible. Our knowledge of God involves the Holy Spirit being in us, not in a way whereby the Spirit ceases to be God, but in a way whereby we get to know God. We get to know God, not just in the flesh, but through the Spirit.

The Holy Spirit is our knowledge of God.; not only because the Spirit is a *means* of knowledge, but because in the Spirit, we have God. God the Spirit works within us, drawing us into deeper knowledge. And the Spirit is not just the agent of knowledge, the Spirit is the content of knowledge. The Spirit also helps us distinguish between God and ourselves. As the Spirit works within us, we recognize that we are being turned to God; that it is God self-revealing, not us simply growing in self-knowledge. The more we get to know the Spirit, the more we get to know God, and the less we think we are the same as God. As the Spirit comes to meet us, we see the extent of our need; we see that we cannot get to God without the Spirit. Therein lies the difference: On our own, we do not *know* God; we don't have God. When we come to know God, we do so as recipients—recipients of the divine Spirit.

Why I find this so helpful is that in encountering God, I feel as though I am getting the real deal. Despite myself, I believe it is God who I am getting to know. And it turns out that this is not a vain hope. God is not trying to pull the wool over our eyes. God does not want us to know a lesser version of him. God wants to be known so much that the Spirit—who is God—lives within us. And this relates to feeling. We feel as though the Spirit works within us. We feel love, joy, longing, and grief. Yes, these are human emotions, but we experience them because of what God is doing in us.

In Spirit encounter, in Spirit adoption, we not only receive God's touch; we not only chance upon God's presence. In the Spirit, we have God with us *now*—in the moment. God's presence with us and within us is for our salvation, for our transformation, but it is also personal. It feels personal because it is. That is why we desire times like these. We are not getting to know everything there is to know about God. God remains distinct, but it is God that we are getting. Our minds might not be prepared for such knowledge, but the Spirit helps us in our weakness.

Our reception of Christ is likewise an event of knowing. When we read about Christ in Scripture, when we feast on bread and wine, when we contemplate Christ's incarnation, we conclude that God is there. We get God in Jesus. We agree with Jesus when he says "Whoever has seen me has seen the Father," not just because we believe Christ is of the same substance as the Father, but because as we behold Jesus, as we receive Jesus, there is an event of knowing. Something is happening. It is not only the disciples that see Jesus and get the Father. It is still true for us. It is not that Jesus only shows something, that in the human face of Jesus we only get a glimpse. He means more. When we receive Jesus, we receive God.

We must not think that there is in fact a true God behind Jesus: a fuller and more complete version, or that Jesus is protecting us from this God for fear of us becoming consumed or confused. As already suggested, we should not imagine that when Jesus says "Whoever has seen me has seen the Father," he was having us on. We shouldn't think his statement contains certain terms and conditions in small type that would secure God's freedom. Jesus did not say, "Whoever has seen me has had a partial glimpse of the mystery that is God the Father." He doesn't hold back. And we have seen Jesus: in word, deed, and meal. In these events, we are coming into the knowledge of God. We are entering into the throne room of God's presence.

This is full-bodied knowledge. It comes in all grace, but is not therefore diminished. It is not watered down. I recognize my inability to possess God on my own terms, but knowledge is mine nonetheless. It is a mystery, for sure, but it is not *only* a mystery. It is a mystery that we might be recipients of such kindness, but as we come to know the kindness giver, as we do in these events, we are not so surprised that it has happened.

2

The Knowing God

Vulnerable God

NOT SO LONG AGO, there was a movement in theology towards emphasizing God's suffering. Not only does God relate to us personally, but he also enters into the depths of what it is to suffer. Jürgen Moltmann is the best-known advocate of this view.[1] Moltmann builds on the provocative statement of Dietrich Bonhoeffer from his prison cell, "Only the suffering God can help."[2] Responses to Moltmann have been varied, not least in evangelical circles. I have been in contexts where Moltmann's theology has been introduced for the first time. For some, there is a lightbulb moment. God cares enough to suffer. Everything falls into place around this realization. For others, a warning light flashes on. God is not meant to suffer. God is meant to be the same yesterday, today, and forever. Whatever we make of it, Moltmann seems to offer a new way of talking about God. Saying God suffers recognizes the closeness of God's relationship to us humans. God is close enough to be affected.

When I first reflected on the possibility of God's suffering, it moved me to tears, particularly as certain people came to mind. I knew people who had known real suffering. Yes, Moltmann's theology raised questions, but there were clearly positive implications: God cares; God cares enough to suffer. The experience of God in the world was not removed from my acquaintances and friends who had suffered. The pain felt in the Godhead meant that their pain was not only their own. I felt the weight of this when spending time with people who had suffered at the hands of others: refugees;

1. It is the central theme of Moltmann's *Crucified God.*
2. Bonhoeffer, *Letters and Papers*, 361.

victims of gang violence and abuse; those pushed into circumstances they had not chosen for themselves. That God would be in solidarity with these people struck me as a remarkable thing.

It is arguably biblical to talk about the suffering of God. No one denies that Scripture can talk about God as deeply personal: Take Ezekiel's words: "I passed by you again and looked on you; you were at the age for love. I spread the edge of my cloak over you, and covered your nakedness: I pledged myself to you and entered into a covenant with you, says the Lord God, and you became mine."[3] The language is tender in the extreme. But there is more. Suffering is not excluded from this personal relation. Later in the same chapter, when Israel has been unfaithful, God responds. And the response looks like it comes from the place of having been affected. God is furious, jealous, and enraged.[4]

The God of Scripture, says Moltmann, enters so personally into our affairs that he suffers. God is not absolute power, detached from the world. Instead, God shows power through weakness. This is nowhere more profound than in the godforsaken cry of Jesus on the cross: "My God, my God why have you forsaken me."[5] This is not a simple separation of Father and Son, in the sense of the Father turning his back on the Son. Rather, forsakenness is undertaken by God himself. It is a forsakenness of the Trinity. In the cross, Jesus' agony is not only his. Yes, Jesus goes it alone. There is an abandonment here. But this aloneness is not only his—Father and Spirit feel it too. Moltmann puts it starkly. The cry of dereliction from the cross expresses "My God, why has thou forsaken *thyself*."[6] God knows forsakenness.

For Moltmann, God is a suffering God, but not only as a victim. God *actively* draws suffering into himself. Some of those I knew who had experienced forsakenness were Christians. They knew also the forsaken cry of Christ. It meant something to them. But God's suffering does not stop our suffering. Rather, it speaks something into suffering: it speaks hope into hopelessness, love into brokenness, healing into pain.

It would be easy to reject Moltmann's work. He denies God's impassibility—the belief that God cannot experience pain or other emotions at

3. Ezek 16:8.

4. Ezek 16:42–43.

5. Matt 27:46. Jesus' cry of dereliction is central to Moltmann's point. See particularly *Crucified God*, 147–55.

6. Moltmann, *Crucified God*, 153.

the hands of others. He also seems to deny immutability—the doctrine of God's unchanging nature. I don't want to analyze these doctrinal areas closely. However, like Moltmann, I recognize how very personal God is. Saying that God suffers communicates genuine personhood. To suffer with someone is to really know them. Are we okay talking about a God who desires a relationship so much that he will suffer with us? Surely we are. Is this God open to us to the point of change? We can answer yes to the first question without having to say yes to the second. If we go too far in allowing for God's susceptibility to pain—if we talk as though God is *affected*, as Moltmann does, then we are questioning divine freedom—God's freedom to be God. Regardless of whether Moltmann is guilty of this, I don't want to be. That is why *how* we talk about God's freedom is so important.[7]

A way through is to emphasize God's vulnerability over God's suffering. God acts in vulnerability rather than as the victim. God is proactive rather than reactive. Following Barth, William Placher opts for such language. In freedom, God has chosen vulnerability. God's freedom is not at stake in the same way as our freedom is when we suffer. God's divinity is not at stake. So Barth: "God is moved and stirred, yet not like ourselves in powerlessness, but in His own free power, in His innermost being."[8] God's movement towards us, God's identification with us, God's active suffering *for* us, is born out of his free decision.

Being a victim of suffering is not good. To say that God is the victim is to draw what is not good into God. God acts in love, acts in freedom, acts in vulnerability; but God is not at the mercy of evil. If God suffers, it is not as the one who is overcome by the evil of the world. This is the difference between love and evil. Evil demands suffering; love is revealed in vulnerability—revealed in freedom. Vulnerability, chosen, is good. This is what we see happen in the cross. The Son enters into it in loving freedom. It is agonizing, abhorrent, and dreadful, but is born out of the freedom of love, not out of the demand of evil. As Placher says, "love does not regret the price it pays for making itself vulnerable, but to speak of paying a price is in itself to acknowledge that the suffering itself is an evil. Vulnerability, on the other hand, is a perfection of loving freedom."[9] Christ's suffering on the cross, in other words, judges evil as evil and love as love.

---

7. Moltmann is aware of the problem. However, he argues that it is our understanding of the nature of divine freedom that needs adjustment. See Moltmann, *Trinity*, 56.

8. Barth in Placher, *Narratives of a Vulnerable God*, 19.

9. Placher, *Narratives of a Vulnerable God*, 19.

God's loving vulnerability says he knows us in our vulnerability and wills to be known. Here is a God who walks the extra mile; who tracks down and finds the lost sheep; who suffers crucifixion for those he loves. God is not only a heroic savior, but a companion and friend. This is the God we find moving towards the wayward son: "But while he was still far off, his father saw him and was filled with compassion; he ran and put his arms around him and kissed him."[10] God is full of compassion; and this compassion relates at least in part to what God sees in us. It is not *just* an attribute of God; it is something God allows himself to feel. And God does not bestow this compassion from far off. God does everything for us, but also alongside us, with us, and in us. In all this, God does not cease to be God. In fact, God is being God, because God is love.

When I first read Moltmann, I thought a shift would need to happen were I to accept what he says. But it is not such a shift if we are careful with our language. His point is not so polemical—certainly no more radical than the Gospels allow Jesus to be. Indeed he does no more than agree with Charles Wesley's great hymn: "Amazing love! how can it be, that Thou, my God, shouldst die for me."[11] To recognize the vulnerable God might overturn our preheld views, but it is there in Scripture. We are merely stating that this God cares. Care—love—takes the form of what it cares for. It is not love if there is no involvement—if it is distant. This is the love that we have in God.

As I reflect on the vulnerability of God, I see the implications for how I approach others. It inclines me towards vulnerability in love. It pushes me towards those as broken as I am, with the hope that I won't lose myself when coming alongside them. To be destroyed by others would not be love. To take on everyone's burdens to the point whereby I can no longer operate as me is not love. It is victimhood. It is abuse. To move towards people in vulnerability *is* love. For this movement to arise from being in the image of the God who moves towards us, is love. To suffer with others is love. Of course, I do not do this in a divine way. The risk is less for me. My ability to love is not the same. But what I see in God allows me to walk with others, giving a precedent for care. It says that when I actively allow myself to feel the pain of others, it is not as a victim but as God's companion in the world.

10. Luke 15:20.
11. Charles Wesley, 1738. Public Domain.

Noncompetitive God

When it comes to knowing God, grace is everything. In my church tradition, teaching on grace has been foundational.[12] It means that when thinking about God, I cannot help but think about grace. We know God because we have received something. We have received an unmerited gift. In the first part, our focus was the Word become flesh. This is pure gift. In the second part, I said that the Spirit is likewise gift. When we experience the Spirit within us, we experience something given, not generated. What this means is that God does not want us to jump through hoops to reach him. We do not have to be exceptional, or stand out. Similarly, we need not get ahead of others to get to God. It is not as though God's presence only comes to those who are first over the winning line. Also, God does not force himself upon us. This unmerited gift we receive does not come against us. God does not jostle for our attention. God might deserve our attention and our adoration, but it is not out of a deep-seated need in God that we are required to worship. God does not need stoking up. God is not attention-seeking in the way we normally understand it. If God demands it, then it is best for us. God wants us to worship for *our* sake, not his.

Unsurprisingly, I have taught many children who are attention-seeking. They compete with each other to stand out, whether it be through over-performing, misbehaving, or courting disaster. If one child puts their hand up in class, another will put theirs up higher. When they receive their tests back, they want to know whether they have done better (or worse) than their peers. We all do it. We long to be noticed. As adults, we become subtler—more adept at masking our craving for attention. Sometimes, we develop a false humility, which is just as attention-seeking as brazen confidence. I still find it difficult if my view is not taken into consideration at work or in a meeting at church. I want people to notice my contribution, to value it, and to tell me that they value it. I would often rather people be persuaded by me than by someone else about the same thing. I know how wrong this is, but it still happens. God, thank goodness, is not like this. God hasn't a sycophantic bone in his body.

Put differently, a great deal of modern life is about competition. This affects the worlds of education, business, markets, politics, and more besides. Wealth generation comes through competition in the market: the

---

12. This owes a great deal to Terry Virgo, the founder of Newfrontiers, and his teaching on grace. See, for example, Virgo, *Enjoying God's Grace*.

selling and buying of stocks; lending; interest; and profit. Life is good for the winners, but bad for the losers. The winners get to stand out over and above everyone else. The problem with standing out over others is what happens to the others. For one person to rise, another must fall or be pushed down. Added to this is the cult of celebrity that floods our media platforms. To stay in the public eye, one has to be ever more popular, more scandalous, or more controversial. Competing for attention is the disturbing norm. When we receive attention, it is again at the expense of others. If we push ourselves into the public eye, we leave others in the shadows.

Kathryn Tanner says that God's relation to us is noncompetitive.[13] It is a remarkable assertion—challenging, but wholly appropriate. It is utterly countercultural. All God is—powerful; loving; knowing; gracious— he is without wanting us to be anything less than we are. Nothing God does is done at our expense, or at our loss. God does not try to stand out through impressiveness, nor brag of his achievements. In this way, God is very unlike my students, unlike the markets, unlike celebrity culture, and just as unlike me.

Even God at his most ferocious, most brutal, most destructive, is not driven by competition. He is driven by love. I have long found the narrative of the plagues born by Egypt troubling; that God would meter out such terror on those he has created. But God is not seeking to destroy to show that he is the boss. Pharaoh gets opportunity after opportunity. The first act is not one of violence. Moses' staff turns into a snake; even the snake is not after destruction to begin with. God wants his people to be set free—liberated. God's action is born out of a desire for the liberation of his covenant people. This makes the story no less troubling, but it shows that God is not out to get the Egyptians. Pharaoh has pitched himself against God, but God is not interested in pitching himself against Pharaoh, even less belittling the Egyptians. It is only for the sake of solidarity with his persecuted people— for their freedom—that God does these things.

There are implications for us. When God comes into our lives, it is not in a way that belittles us. None of this means we should make much of ourselves. Indeed, at our end, we would do well to make everything of God. It may be a Godly attitude to approach God through self-effacement, but God's love is not conditional on such an attitude. When John the Baptist says "you must increase, but I must decrease," he is not setting a precedent

13. Tanner, *Jesus, Humanity, and the Trinity*, 2–4.

for how God treats his creatures.[14] In one sense, we can say we want to give God more space in our lives; but equally, God does not want to force us out to make room for himself. God does not belittle us when he comes to us. John makes way for Jesus, but he is not saying that Jesus' coming undermines his ministry. Jesus doesn't see the need to push him out. Lest we forget, Herod was the one to push John out, not Jesus.

A disclaimer: Although I can be competitive, more usually I find competitiveness oppressive. I sometimes balk when I see people being ultra-competitive. It makes me want to play the fool, or even retreat, rather than step up to the mantle. I am sure this is as much a character flaw in me as it is a strength. It may well mean that because of my predisposition, I find a noncompetitive God more appealing. But I still think Tanner is on to something. What I am contending for is pushing back against the need to outdo, the need to see this as good. We don't see it in God; why put it on each other?

Granted, there are perfectly good Darwinian explanations for our disposition towards competition, even our need to be ultra-competitive. I don't disagree with these explanations. But in the light of grace, of unmerited favor, of compassion and gentleness, I find the aggressiveness of Darwinism a problem. Competition, at the very least, is not wholly good—not eternally good. By saying God is noncompetitive, I am not trying to rob his glory or deny that God is majestic and victorious. It is just that he is not these things at our expense.

God's default position is love. God's greatness includes a lack of need to push himself on us. Not that we can be excused for neglecting God. Indeed, our source of life is God. We are only really ourselves when we are engaged in worship of God. As much as we have a relationship of reciprocity with God, we cannot forget its origin in God's creative act. A mother's relationship with her child is reciprocal, but this same mother might be the source of her child's life. The child comes *from* the mother. The child does not generate their own life. Just so with us children in relation to God. Thus, the Prophet Isaiah, "Shall I open the womb and not deliver? says the Lord."[15] God delivers us children as one having gone through labor, as a mother. But a mother does not vie for the child's attention. She gives the child attention because it is good for the child. So too with God. The mother does not outdo the child, suppress the child, or belittle the child. To

14. John 3:30

15. Isa 66:9.

refer to Isaiah once again, "as a mother comforts her child, so I will comfort you."[16] This is God's way with people. We do not instigate such a relationship with God; but a relationship with God is ours nonetheless. God relates to us for our sake.

> This non-competitive relation between creatures and God is possible, it seems, only if God is fecund provider of *all* that the creature is in itself; the creature in its giftedness, in its goodness, does not compete with God's gift-fullness and goodness because God is the giver of all that the creature is for the good.[17]

There is a lot in this. If our lives are from God, we can trust that God is for our good. God is not against us. Further, we cannot *make* God pleased with us. What is pleasing in us is from God anyway. We cannot earn God's respect. We need not do more to stand out and be noticed by God. Everything that we are is from him. Yes, gratitude should be our default position, but this does not add to God.

When we wonder what it means to worship God, we can just as much think it is to love others as to direct praise heavenwards. After all, this is how God has loved us. In this way we bring honor to God. Yes, we should adore God, but out of gratitude more than compulsion. If we love others, then we don't stand out from them or over them. If we love others, we love what God loves and thus love God in them. This has implications for worship as a collective act. When we come together, we do so for each other and thus for God. This is why Paul says: "When you come together, each one has a hymn, a lesson, a revelation, a tongue, or an interpretation. Let all things be done for building up."[18] He doesn't mean "building up" as in being better. He means building up together, for the sake of relationship, for the sake of bringing honor to the God of love. The sense of this comes into view when we are reminded that God is not competitive. That is why worship is cooperative; mutual; joyful. It is not, "who has the best word from God?" We know this, but when competition fades, the temptation to impress also fades.

In our relating to God, we can put competitiveness to rest. We need not compete for God's attention. Christ is for us not because we have caught his attention, but because of who he is. We do not realize, sometimes, how much competitiveness is written into us: into our play, work, and service in

16. Isa 66:13.
17. Tanner, *Jesus, Humanity and the Trinity*, 3.
18. 1 Cor 14:26.

God's community. We are victims of a world of competition. But it is not God's way. Just because elsewhere everything is about competition, it need not be amongst the church. Likewise, our understanding of God, need not be shaped by it. Tanner continues, "In the final analysis, God does not so much want something *of* us as want to be *with* us. God does not really need us *for* anything. There is nothing yet to achieve beyond what God's own Trinitarian perfection already instantiates."[19] God does not need to achieve anything. Nevertheless, God wants to be with us. I find this liberating. God is not in it to get something out of me. And this is cause for praise. As I think about the shape of our lives: what we devote our time to; what we set our minds upon, it can so often be on achieving something. God's state of having nothing to achieve means that his heart is set on love: on love according to his Triune self, and on entering into loving relationship with his children. As we come into this love, as we experience it amongst us, our desires are likewise turned away from the need to achieve, and towards the needs of each other.

In one sense, God demands everything of us, but not because he *needs* something from us. He demands everything because it is best for us. What God desires for himself is to be *with* us. That is every bit as scandalous as it sounds. And God is not waiting for us so to respond to him so he can be vindicated or bolstered. As Tanner says, there is nothing left for God to achieve.

It is sobering to think God doesn't need us. It is even more sobering when we realize God nevertheless wants us. And this relates to the knowledge of God. God's desire is for us, meaning that his want is also for us to know him. God's lack of need likewise speaks of God's freedom to be known. The freedom of not needing to achieve anything is a powerful thing. It means that God's action comes from a desire for us, resulting in God's wanting to be known *by* us.

To know God, we need to change, but knowledge does not come easily, or even naturally. We need the incarnation of the Word. We need God with us. Because of the deep problem of our sin, and our brokenness, a radical breaking into our situation was necessary. Tanner recognizes that, as much as God does not want to fight us into submission, there is a struggle; the incarnation is not smooth sailing. The road to our liberation is bumpy for God, for Christ. We only need look at the cross to see this. Here is an act of extreme violence directed against the Son of God. The cross is God's bearing of the violence of the world. Christ disestablishes the need of the world to

---

19. Tanner, *Jesus, Humanity and the Trinity*, 68.

dominate, to subjugate, to win. God's way of dealing with this is not through violent retaliation or counter-dominance. The victory of the cross is a strange one, not recognizable through any criteria of victory we have today. There is a battle being fought, but it is not one for God's supremacy, it is one for our freedom; our liberation. "The Word's assuming or bearing of all this in Christ means a fight with it, a fight whose success is assured by that very unity of the human with the Word, but a genuine fight nonetheless where success is not immediate but manifests itself over the course of time."[20]

As much as the becoming man of God involves a battle, it does not follow that it is God subjecting us to his will. The fight is *for* us, not against us. That the Son would unite his divine nature to our human nature is intended from eternity. It comes straight from the heart of God. God's desire is to become human with us. Therefore, God is not forcing himself on us. He is coming alongside us; entering into the world *with* us. It displays a love for humanity at its most full, the same love that created us in the first place; the same love that will complete in us what it started.

If we say that God's relation to us is noncompetitive, then we need not fear for his sanctity. Being given to humanity—being vulnerable—these things are not problematic if we do not make hierarchy the basis of power. Tanner is very insistent on this. We think we do justice to God by putting him at the top of the hierarchy—by idolizing him. It is strange, because we know idolatry is wrong. But anything that turns something into an idol, even if it is God, makes of that thing something it is not. There is a fine line between idolatry and worship. But God has not put himself on a pedestal. Jesus has put himself with us: with the vulnerable, with the broken. He can do this because in doing so he is not contradicting his nature. God acts in freedom as the one who is the essence of love. And this is also how God would be known: not at the top, nor even at the bottom, but in the middle; for and with us, not against us, not in competition with us. We think we do God justice by insisting upon his absolute Lordship. True, but not if we disallow his freedom to come to us; not if we disallow God's willingness to condescend himself to be with us in love.

Omniscient God

We are accustomed to saying that God is omniscient—all-knowing. Omniscience seems fundamental to Christian description of God. What does it

20. Tanner, *Jesus, Humanity and the Trinity*, 28.

mean? We can start by saying what it does not mean. It does not mean that God is a know-it-all, or that God is nosey. It does not mean that God is like "big-brother," always looking down on us to check up on what we are getting up to, or looking into our deepest thoughts. So how does God know? More importantly, how does God know us? God's omniscience is personal. When God knows, it is knowledge in love. God doesn't know in a way that belittles us or for the sake of knowing more than us. This follows from what I have said about God's noncompetitive relation to us. God's knowledge is for us and is thus personal. Kathryn Sonderegger encapsulates the essence of such personal knowledge: "God's Perfect Knowledge, that is, must extend to the act of "seeing through our eyes." Entering so fully into creaturely ways that the Creator knows "from the inside" what our very being is like.[21] This is knowing from within; knowing what it is like to be as we are, knowing what it is like to feel as we do. Surely this is the best way of knowing.

Omniscience can sometimes be abstracted from Jesus. We somehow see it as a property of the Father, or worse, a property of deity, forgetting that God is Trinity. God knows in Christ, not in abstraction. Putting it in even more personal terms, "the Lord God rather knows in a first-personal and inward way who I am, and the reach and texture of my inner world . . . He knows the very fabric of my soul."[22] Sonderegger is not saying that God becomes human so he can know what it feels like. It is not as though Jesus was lacking the experience and therefore the knowledge of being human, prior to his incarnation. Some of my students think this is the essence of the incarnation: God getting to know what it is like to be us. God doesn't *need* to get to know us in the sense of needing to add to his catalogue of knowledge. Nevertheless, God's way with humanity includes knowing from the inside. God's eternal way of knowing includes his eternal will to become human. This is omniscience. Thus, omniscience is not so much a philosophical definition, but more the lived existence of God in Christ.

In knowing us in this way—that is, personally, and inwardly—God's being is not at stake. God does not lose himself through union with us. So, Sonderegger again: "He does not exhaust Himself in His descent down into the dust of this realm, so He does not forsake His Liberty and Life to withhold, to withdraw, to resist and refrain, to exhibit the marks of the personal."[23] God's closeness to us in Christ does not endanger his freedom.

21. Sonderegger, *Doctrine of God*, 359.
22. Sonderegger, *Doctrine of God*, 360.
23. Sonderegger, *Doctrine of God*, 361.

God *could* draw away, but doesn't. The choice to draw close is personal, born out of desire for us, not out of necessity.

So, if God's reason for coming to us is not for the purpose of knowing more, what is it? God's reason is relationship. Although God is not lacking in knowledge, his knowledge relates to knowing us personally. Again, this confirms the noncompetitive manner of God's way with us. God's knowledge, that is, does not happen at our expense. God's knowing us is for our sake. It is also the basis for our knowledge of God. How God knows is revealed to us because God knows relationally. In knowing us through relationship, we know something of God through this same relationship. God's knowing enables our knowing. We know through being known. How does this happen? Through the ways we have talked about so far: through Christ's incarnation; through life in the Spirit. Christ's coming is an event of God's omniscience. The incarnation is God's very personal way of knowing, which, in turn, opens up our knowledge of God. We know God for who he is in Christ. The Spirit's outpouring, too, is an event of God's omniscience; an event of the all-knowing God *for* us; an event of *personal* knowing. And as God comes, as we encounter, we receive personal knowledge of this one who knows us to the core; knows what it is to be like us; knows what it is to be living in us.

Yes, God knows every hair on our head. But that is not as important as the fact that he knows what it is to be with us. I feel God knows me. And my hope for this is that his life in Christ looks like knowing people like us. He gets to know a band of followers who also get to know him. He knew them before, but this knowing is manifest in his getting to know them then. He is interested in their present. God is for our now. When reading the Gospels, in particular, I can picture myself with this Jesus, being drawn to him, sharing life with him—all as an act of grace, but nonetheless reciprocally, in friendship, and in a way where I am not diminished and he is not compromised.

The best way of illustrating God's closeness to us, including God's wanting to be known, is by focusing on those whom he calls to friendship; in particular, the band of twelve who had the honor of God's time in Jesus.

3

He Comes as One to be Known

A Sermon

John 1:35–39 NLT

[35]The following day John was again standing with two of his disciples. [36]As Jesus walked by, John looked at him and declared, "Look! There is the Lamb of God!" [37]When John's two disciples heard this, they followed Jesus.

[38]Jesus looked around and saw them following. "What do you want?" he asked them.

They replied, "Rabbi" (which means "Teacher"), "where are you staying?"

[39]"Come and see," he said. It was about four o'clock in the afternoon when they went with him to the place where he was staying, and they remained with him the rest of the day.

What Do You Want?

"WHAT DO YOU WANT?" If you could have anything, what would you have? Most people's wants are similar. We want stuff: shelter; food; clothes. We want relationships: love; friendship; intimacy. We want a purpose: a vocation; a task; fulfillment. We need most of these things. It is good to want. It is human to want. Wanting, desiring, it tends to come from God.[1]

Admittedly, we sometimes want the wrong things. We can want what others have, when we haven't. We can want immediate gratification at the

---

1. The sermon idea came from the theme of James K. Smith's *You Are What You Love*.

expense of what will be of long-term benefit. We often want things that are bad for us. We can be greedy, selfish, lustful, and gluttonous. We can even want to hurt people. This is what we want gone wrong.

Jesus' question, "What do you want?," is challenging for anyone. It is so direct. So, what do we want—for ourselves, for our loved ones, for the world? People say they want many things. But what are our deepest, best wants? What do we *want* to want? We have to listen hard to ourselves to know what we really want. We have to listen *really* hard if we want to know what others want.

As John would have it, Jesus delights in asking people questions. We could learn a lot from this. Love asks questions. Real engagement comes through dialogue. We have a message to share, but just as importantly, we want to hear people—take an interest in people. We like answers, but maybe having questions is better. As a family, we took the plunge and purchased a big brand virtual assistant. Speak a question and get an immediate answer; what could be better? There is no shortage of answers in the modern world. The Internet has long given us immediate knowledge. But Jesus doesn't ask questions because he wants to know the answer. He asks questions to generate desire, to enable people to express want.

What do John's disciples want from Jesus? Money, friendship, a job? Their answer is, "Where are you staying?" They answer a question with a question. It is a funny thing to say, but what does it mean? It seems like they want to get to know Jesus. That is the nub. Isn't that what we all want—to know Jesus? I do. More broadly, don't we long to know *and* be known? Sometimes it is said that for emotional fulfillment we need two things: to be known, and to be accepted once known. Whoever we are, whatever we have done, whatever we have been through, we want acceptance.

Clearly, there is something about Jesus in particular that makes them want to go with him. Maybe it was because John says he is the Lamb of God. I am not even sure they would have known what John meant. They might have hoped Jesus was the promised Messiah. They might just have been bored with John. Maybe John was trying to get rid of them: "Look, the lamb of God" he says, as he runs off the other way! We don't know the reason for sure. What we can say is that Jesus' invitation results in them following him. They want to be with him.

He responds to their "where are you staying?" with "come and see." Finally, someone answers a question! What an invitation. Come to my place. Come to where I am. This is a real honor—being invited in by the teacher—the Rabbi. It is almost as though he is saying "come and be a part of the family." It is that personal. Jesus gives them his time, his undivided attention.

Time

In Jesus, God has given us his time. Usually, we say God is outside of time. Philosophers love to ponder such things. But more interesting than God's being outside of time is his entering into our time. God enters into time in Jesus. This is real love. God takes time into himself. And in today's passage, we see that Jesus literally gives the disciples his time. We must not think that when Jesus gives them his time, it is not God's time. He is not just giving them time with a human face. He is not giving them time as an act of condescension, as though only to make them think he cares. The time he gives comes from his heart for them. Jesus is giving them—us—the time of God.

One of the most powerful things we can do for people is to give them our time. I love my time. If I know all my time will be taken away from me or given to something I haven't chosen, I get grouchy. I don't like my time being planned for me. It is my form of introversion, I guess. I want to do what I want to do when I want to do it! Although this disposition of mine is not godly, it highlights something. It highlights that time is precious, whilst admitting time is broken. We frequently see the brokenness of time. We experience the feeling of not having enough time. Some hate being rushed. Some struggle to make it to places on time. Some struggle when people are late! Time pressures can make us stressed. We don't like our time being wasted. We give our time to useless things. These things reveal the brokenness of time. It means that giving each other quality time is difficult. However, most of us think it is worth it. We certainly appreciate it when others give us their time.

Verse 39 says they "went with him." "Went with" is literal. Jesus invites them to go with him and be with him where he is staying. It is an invitation to see who Jesus is—to get to know him. Jesus offers himself as he is. He doesn't say "come round later," so he can get back and put the pots in the dishwasher before they arrive. The invite is for now. What an invitation.

Just what is God offering us in Jesus? He is offering us himself. And the offer is for this moment. We can jump to other lessons in the passage: we could learn from the disciple's willingness to go with Jesus. Maybe we can locate the start of the church here and talk about that. These things are here, but more importantly, this is an invitation from God. Jesus invites us to himself. God wants to know us and for us to know him. In Jesus, we get God. Jesus says this himself: "Whoever has seen me has seen the Father."[2] I don't think all of this had dawned on the disciples at this moment, but it would do later.

Of course, it is clear we can follow Jesus without understanding him. Lots of people see Jesus as the good teacher. They might be happy to follow him if he asked them. That is where it starts. The disciples did not understand much to begin with but were willing to give him a shot. But although they don't know him much yet, it is still Jesus that they are getting. Just because they don't see what it will mean for them to follow doesn't mean that Jesus is not willing. There is still much that we find mysterious about this man, but it doesn't follow that he is holding something back.

Today, Jesus would be amongst those least likely to enter the church. They would be his followers. He would call those on the fringes: addicts, rough sleepers, travelers. Wouldn't it be great to have such people in our churches? Sometimes we make the call to follow Jesus too complicated; so complicated that some feel as though they cannot come with us. However, to be a follower of Jesus starts with a simple "going with." We sometimes put things in people's way, but Jesus would not have it so. We most likely didn't swallow the gospel whole before getting on the bus with him. Why expect this of others?

But that is not the end of the matter. Jesus does not just want hangers on; he wants more for us than clinging on with our fingertips. John tells us that they "remained with him" for the rest of the day. Remain is literal, but powerfully metaphorical. Yes, they physically stayed with him for the rest of the day. But more significantly, they shifted their priorities for the sake of what he offered. Being a disciple of Jesus is not just following, it is remaining. It means crossing over a line into wanting to know him more. We may not understand everything, but at some point we need to *want* to get to know Jesus and be willing to be transformed by the experience. We cannot forever know partially from the sidelines. He is offering more than that. And on the back of his offer, we are to throw our lot in, and be faithful to him until the end. If you are on the sidelines, please step in; it couldn't be more worth it.

2. John 14:9.

Accepting Jesus is not a one-off affair. It is not an "I feel like this today, so I'm going to go with it" kind of thing. Jesus is not after a merely emotive response. As soon as he says "Come and see," he is committing himself to the long haul. Are we? The invitation is just the start. Jesus is calling us into so much more. It is a major honor to be called by Jesus. It amounts to an invitation to join his family for eternity. It is a "remain" relationship. Relationships are rarely "remain" in modern life. Like many other things, they have a shelf life. We are used to discarding things when we have worn them out, whether it be clothes, food, or even relationships. We live in an age of disposability. This is bad for the environment and bad for our understanding of God. The gospel says something different. It speaks permanence. God's will in Christ towards us is an offer of eternal friendship. It is not disposable.

Friendship

The Christian God is the friendship of Father, Son and Holy Spirit. When Jesus offers his friendship, he offers the eternal love of God. God wants us for friends. What could be better? It is all we could ever wish for. But it is not purely sentimental. I am not advocating a warm and fuzzy Christianity with no discipleship—no cost. This friendship is gutsy, demanding, and sacrificial. Being friends with us costs Jesus.[3] It involves him leaving the majesty in heaven to become flesh. It involves the cross. That means we cannot sentimentalize this particular friendship. What we can say, is that the cost of it makes it unbreakable.

Jesus, the incarnation of the Word, seeks people out in friendship. He leaves his throne to seek it. He seeks the lost, not just to bestow kindness, but to give himself fully. The eternal Son wants to be known, wants Father and Spirit to be known. This would all be a massive risk for God, were it not what he is about. There is something about God—something about his character—that is wired for friendship. It is integral to his being. And it is not that God needs us as friends. God gives himself to genuine friendship because he *wants* us as friends.

We too are designed for friendship—friendship with God and friendship with each other. It is what we most deeply long for. If you were to ask someone—anyone—whether they can think of anything more important than friendship, they would be hard pushed. Hence, what do we *really*

---

3. As Bonhoeffer famously states at the start of his *Discipleship*, "Cheap grace is the moral enemy of our church. Our struggle today is for costly grace" (43).

want? We really want friendship. It is a gift, a joy, a challenge. Friendship with God is an unlikely thing when we consider what we are like. It is not so unlikely when we consider what God is like. When we look at Jesus, we must see this. We can dare hope that God wants to be known—wants friendship. We will need to change, but the invitation comes first. God's "yes" comes first.

Augustine said "you only love your friend truly, after all, when you love God in your friend, either because he is in him, or in order that he may be in him."[4] Love—friendship—is from God. That is why we see God in others when we love them even if they do not recognize God. When we love someone, whoever they may be, we reflect God's love to them. We invite them into something. This is the good news, the gospel, and hence the birthplace of mission. As God loves in friendship, so we love in friendship.

You have heard it said that the only certainties are "death and taxes." The gospel is more hopeful. It promises eternal friendship: friendship with God, and friendship with others, now and for eternity. Death and taxes just happen. Friendship that lasts needs embracing; it must be actively pursued. And friendship is worth pursuing—worth embracing. It is the most important thing we can have—the best thing we can devote our lives to.

However, friendship is broken. We have all known broken friendships. Friendship is also hard work. Many carry past pain. Some of us need the scars of broken friendship healing. Whether it is friendship with God or friendship with others, we can find it difficult to throw ourselves in because of what we have experienced. It is true that friendship involves a risk. It is true that we might be hurt again. But it only needs to start with an invitation: "Come and see." That is the first step: towards friendship; towards wholeness of life; towards reconciliation. God has given us his time—given us himself. We can say we are friends of God. God in Christ has invited you to "come and see." You go to others, then, and do likewise.

4. Quoted in Hacker, *Passions*, 329.

God for Now

Conclusion

I STILL FIND MYSELF wanting to be Christian each day. Evangelical and charismatic? Sure, why not? Yes, I have acknowledged the questions I have had with my faith heritage. Occasionally I have been critical. But we needn't throw the baby out with the bathwater. The tradition still holds so much: A relentless focus on the chief character—Jesus; a fitting acknowledgement of his companion—the Holy Spirit; an openness to intimacy; to passion; to feeling; a trust in Scripture that says we need not go beyond if we want God. Added to these things, is a vibrancy that says that God is doing something in us today, and wants us to do something.

I hope I haven't reduced theology to experience. What has been set out is a testimony of what it is like to live under the knowledge of God for us now. Longing is matched with reality; desire with hope. Jesus, the same one who walked in history, is God's life for us, seen in speech and deed. Only through believing, through entering in, is the whole of his reality opened up before us, is he understood as the eternal one. But through seeing, through witnessing his presence in Scripture, allegiance becomes both possible and necessary. We need not turn to the Bible into something it isn't in order to accept this. There is enough good news on offer without having to force it. The Bible is not a self-certifying document; nor does it point inwards. Jesus addresses us straight from the pages. He is that real. And as he addresses me, I think, *Why would I not want in?* When he says "Yes, Mark," why would I not follow? This is why I am an evangelical Christian.

Without Jesus, we wouldn't have God. We might have a sense, an idea, but not God in person, not God with us. Thus, any questions that remained are born by this incarnate Word, this enfleshed one. The Son draws our questions and uncertainties into relation with the Father. And the reality of this Son pushes on us now. It feels like something. His vivid presence speaks into my lived existence transformationally, and significantly enough to direct my wants, passions, and priorities. My priorities become joined to his priorities, just as he has joined himself to us. And this means I face out. I look to what this means for others. To understand this is to understand God, because it is where he is looking too.

Could we start theology with Spirit experience? Yes. But it is only a possible move if Christ is there too. It may well be that some will encounter God first through the Spirit. Why shouldn't they? But we can only form an adequate theology of the Spirit when a definite relation with Christ is established. Yet in the Spirit we have someone unique; someone who would not be ours were we only to have the scriptural testament to Christ. We have an imminent relation with God; one in which we are renewed, not just affirmed. One in which we are caught up into God's being with the whole world.

Charismatic Christianity should not be about impressiveness. The phenomena we affirm is no more and no less than a reflection of God's life for the world, in Christ, and in the Spirit. Encounter with the Spirit is thus challenging, and unsettling, as much as it is affirming. And the Christian community, in catching the Spirit, in being where the Spirit chooses to dwell, takes on board the mission of the Spirit. Part of this catching hold is to recognize that the Spirit blows where the Spirt will, not bound to a time or a place. Definitely not bound to a particular way of doing things. And as we live in the Spirit, we can let go of our privileges and step over to the other side—not least the side of others.

God evidently wants to be known: I see it; I feel it. It is a now thing. To say this is not to dishonor him. God is haveable—how outrageous—but how like God. How like God to do everything to make it happen; how like God to do this for our good. How evangelical! God throws himself in. We needed God towards us. We needed salvation; reconciliation; atonement; sanctification, etc., but this movement isn't just an act of condescension. It is God being God. And the extent to which he comes—as the Father of the prodigal, in great vulnerability, with great emotion—is staggering. Not out of the demand of evil, but for the sake of the good; for the sake of us. Not at the expense of us, but for us. As the mother with the child, so God with us.

Although I have not set out a practical theology; a social gospel; an ecclesiology, all these things are here, really. What we have seen in God; what we have received in God, we now live out loud, for the sake of God's community, and for the sake of the world outside the door.

Bibliography

Augustine, Saint. *On the Holy Trinity.* Nicene and Post-Nicene Fathers 3. Edited by Philip Schaff. Reprint, Edinburgh: T. & T. Clark, 1998.

Barth, Karl. *The Doctrine of God, Part 1.* Vol. 2/1 of *Church Dogmatics.* Translated by T. H. L. Parker et al. Edinburgh: T. & T. Clark, 1957.

———. *The Doctrine of God, Part 2.* Vol. 2/2 of *Church Dogmatics.* Translated by Rev. G. W. Bromiley et al. Edinburgh: T. & T. Clark, 1957.

———. *The Doctrine of the Word of God.* Vol. 1/1 of *Church Dogmatics.* Translated by G. T. Thomson et al. Edinburgh: T. & T. Clark, 1936.

———. *Evangelical Theology: An Introduction.* Grand Rapids: Eerdmans, 1979.

Bates, W. Matthew. *Salvation by Allegiance Alone.* Michigan: Baker Academic, 2017.

Bonhoeffer, Dietrich. *Act and Being.* Dietrich Bonhoeffer Works 2. Minneapolis: Fortress, 2009.

———. *Berlin: 1932–1933.* Dietrich Bonhoeffer Works 12. Minneapolis: Fortress, 2009.

———. *Discipleship.* Dietrich Bonhoeffer Works 4. Minneapolis: Fortress, 2001.

———. "Lectures on Christology." In *Berlin,* 299–360. Dietrich Bonhoeffer Works 12. Minneapolis: Fortress, 2009.

———. *Letters and Papers from Prison.* Dietrich Bonhoeffer Works 8. Minneapolis: Fortress, 2010.

Buber, Martin. *I and Thou.* Translated by Walter Kaufmann. New York: Scribner's, 1970.

Calvin, John. *Institutes of the Christian Religion.* Translated by Henry Beveridge. Volume 1. London: James Clark & Co., 1953.

Coakley, Sarah. *God, Sexuality and the Self: An Essay on the "the Trinity."* Cambridge: Cambridge University Press, 2013.

Dahl, Roald. *The BFG.* London: Puffin, 1982.

Dawson, Gerrit. *An Introduction to Torrance Theology.* Edinburgh: T. & T. Clark, 2007.

Deines, Roland. *Acts of God in History: Studies Towards Recovering a Theological Historiography.* Tübingen: Mohr Siebeck, 2013.

Dafydd Jones, Paul. *The Humanity of Christ.* Edinburgh: T. & T. Clark, 2011.

Galli, Mark. "What to Make of Karl Barth's Steadfast Adultery." *Christianity Today,* October 20, 2017. https://www.christianitytoday.com/ct/2017/october-web-only/what-to-make-of-karl-barths-steadfast-adultery.html.

Gollwitzer, Helmut. *Dogmatics in Outline.* Edinburgh: T. & T. Clark, 2000.

Bibliography

Gunton, Colin. *Theology Through the Theologians.* Edinburgh: T. & T. Clark, 1996.

Grudem, Wayne. *Systematic Theology: An Introduction to Biblical Doctrine.* Leicester: InterVarsity, 1994.

Hacker, P. M. S. *The Passions: A Study of Human Nature.* Oxford: Wiley Blackwell, 2018.

Hays, B. Richard. *Reading Backwards.* London: SPCK, 2015.

Hector, W. Kevin. "God's Triunity and Self-Determination: A Conversation with Karl Barth, Bruce McCormack and Paul Molnar." *IJST* 7 (2005) 246–61.

Jensen, Alexander. *Divine Providence and Human Agency: Trinity, Creation and Freedom.* London: Routledge, 2014.

Jeremias, Joachim. *The Proclamation of Jesus.* Vol. 1 of *New Testament Theology.* New Testament Library. London: SCM, 1971.

Kettler, D. Christian. *The God Who Believes: Faith, Doubt and the Vicarious Humanity of Christ.* Eugene, OR: Cascade, 2005.

Kotsko, Adam. "Gift and Communio: The Holy Spirit in Augustine's De Trinitate." *SJT* 64 (2011) 1–12

Lewis, C. S. *The Lion, the Witch and the Wardrobe.* London: Lions, 1950.

Lindsley, Art. "The Importance of Imagination for C.S. Lewis and for Us" http://www.cslewisinstitute.org/webfm_send/277.

McCormack, Bruce. "What Has Basel to Do with Berlin." In *Orthodox and Modern: Studies in the Theology of Karl Barth,* 63–88. Grand Rapids: Baker, 2008.

McNall, Joshua. "Shrinking Pigeon, Brooding Dove: the Holy Spirit in Recent Works by Sarah Coakley and N. T. Wright." *SJT* 69 (2016) 295–308.

McSwain, Jeff. *Movements of Grace: The Dynamic Christo-realism of Barth, Bonhoeffer, and the Torrances.* Eugene, OR: Wipf & Stock, 2010.

Moltmann, Jürgen. *The Crucified God.* London: SCM, 2001.

———. *The Trinity and the Kingdom: The Doctrine of God.* Minneapolis: Fortress, 1993.

Placher, William. *Narratives of a Vulnerable God.* Louisville: Westminster John Knox, 1994.

Piper, John. *Desiring God: Meditations of a Christian Hedonist.* Colorado: Multnomah, 2011.

Schleiermacher, Friedrich. *The Christian Faith.* Louisville: Westminster John Knox, 2016.

Schweitzer, Albert. *The Quest of the Historical Jesus.* 3rd ed. London: A. & C. Black, 1954.

Smith, K. James. *You Are What You Love: The Spiritual Power of Habit.* Grand Rapids: Brazos, 2016.

Spufford, Francis. *Unapologetic: Why, Despite Everything, Christianity Can Still Make Surprising Emotional Sense.* London: Faber & Faber, 2013.

Sonderegger, Katherine. *The Doctrine of God.* Vol. 1 of *Systematic Theology.* Minneapolis: Fortress, 2015.

Tanner, Kathryn. *Christ the Key.* Current Issues in Christology 7. Cambridge: Cambridge University Press, 2009.

———. *Jesus, Humanity and the Trinity: A Brief Systematic Theology.* Minneapolis: Fortress, 2001.

Torrance, Alan. "Can the Truth Be Learned? Redressing the 'Theologistic Fallacy' in Modern Biblical Scholarship." In *Scripture's Doctrine and Theology's Bible: How the New Testament Shapes Christian Dogmatics,* edited by Markus Bockmuehl and Alan Torrance, 143–64. Michigan: Baker Academic, 2008.

Torrance, James. *Worship, Community and the Triune God of Grace.* Leicester: InterVarsity, 1996.

Bibliography

Virgo, Terry. *Enjoying God's Grace*. Eastbourne: Kingsway, 1999.

van der Kooi, Kornelius. *This Incredibly Benevolent force: The Holy Spirit in Reformed Theology and Spirituality*. Grand Rapids: Eerdmans, 2018.

Williams, Rowan. *Christ the Heart of Creation*. London, Bloomsbury Continuum, 2018.

Wilson, Andrew. *Spirit and Sacrament: An Invitation to Eucharismatic Worship*. Grand Rapids: Zondervan, 2018.

Wittgenstein, Ludwig. *Tractatus Logico-Philosophicus*. Routledge Classics. London: Routledge, 2001.

Wright, N. T. *Jesus and the Victory of God*. London: SPCK, 1996.

———. *Paul and the Faithfulness of God*. London: SPCK, 2013.

———. "Jesus and the Identity of God." http://ntwrightpage.com/2016/07/12/jesus-and-the-identity-of-god/.

Lightning Source UK Ltd.
Milton Keynes UK
UKHW021858270520
363925UK00025B/5938